D1488309

A Touch of God

A Touch of God

Eight Monastic Journeys

Edited by
Maria Boulding

with an introduction by
Philip Jebb

ST. BEDE'S PUBLICATIONS
Still River, Massachusetts

First published 1982 by SPCK, London
Copyright © 1982 by The English Benedictine Congregation
This edition is published by arrangement with
Edward England Books, Crowborough, Sussex, Bursar of the
English Benedictine Congregation
All Rights Reserved
PRINTED IN THE UNITED STATES OF AMERICA

LIBRARY OF CONGRESS CATALOGING IN PUBLICATION DATA

Main entry under title:

A Touch of God.

Contents: Wonder is so sudden a gift / Philip Jebb — A
tapestry, from the wrong side / Maria Boulding — Love bade me
welcome / Alan Rees — [etc.]
1. Benedictines—Spiritual life—Addresses, essays, lectures.
2. Monastic and religious life—Addresses, essays, lectures.
3. Benedictine nuns—Spiritual life—Addresses, essays, lectures.
4. Monastic and religious life of women—Addresses, essays,
lectures. I. Boulding, Maria.
BX3003.T68   1983   255'.11   82-24055
ISBN 0-932506-26-7

Contents

ACKNOWLEDGEMENTS

Extracts from the following biblical versions have been used in this publication:

The New English Bible, second edition © 1970, by permission of Oxford and Cambridge University Presses.

The Revised Standard Version of the Bible, copyrighted 1946 and 1952 by the Division of Christian Education of the National Council of the Churches of Christ in the USA.

The Psalms, a translation by The Grail, published in Fontana paperbacks by Collins (1963) and used by permission.

Thanks are also due to the following for permission to quote from copyright sources:

To Macmillan Publishers Ltd: an extract from *Readings in St John's Gospel* by William Temple (1939–40).

To Patrick O'Donovan: 'Great Oaks in the Making', a report first published in the *Catholic Herald*.

Introduction

In January 1979 a group of monks and nuns of the English Benedictine Congregation were asked by Fr Victor Farwell, the Abbot President, to write a book drawing on their monastic experience which could be of interest for the lay reader. It was by no means clear at the outset what kind of book it should be. We spent six months floundering, trying to find the best way to communicate the human and spiritual value of the monastic life to others.

Then one of us felt drawn to write an autobiographical account of his monastic life, and this acted as a catalyst. An atmosphere of trust and understanding grew up in the group and enabled individuals to share something of their inner life. We learned to give without fear and to draw out the best in each other; thus, although each account is personal to the author, it is also the fruit of mutual sympathy and affection. None of us would have felt able to write anything of this sort had we not been encouraged by the others – through support, laughter, criticism and insight.

But this was not simply a work of group therapy, for we came to an awareness that our unity derives from the one God who searches for each of us in a personal and unique way. In particular the honest sharing of some of our failures and weaknesses gave each of us in our different ways a new confidence to face them and to believe that they can be part of the way God is bringing us to wholeness. Indeed, it strengthened our faith that God is real at all: I can sometimes dismiss my own experience of God as a dream, but when I am allowed to accompany others who have grown close to me on their journey, and find the same landmarks, then life takes on a new meaning, and it is God who gives it. The promise of Christ, 'Where two or three of you are gathered in my name, there am I in the midst of you', has been our genuine experience.

We are grateful to Gillian Reynolds, Mary Craig and all those whose sympathetic and positive response encouraged us to persevere in this personal approach. They have convinced us that our experience of hope, fear, joy, friendship and frustration is not purely 'monastic' but human.

This book is published with the support of the General Chapter of the English Benedictine Congregation, but from the nature of the case it remains the expression of the individual writers.

Philip Jebb

Wonder is so Sudden a Gift

DOM PHILIP JEBB

Wonder is so sudden a gift:
Straight from the shooting star,
Or slow dark fishes in pools:
Found in the bursting, toe-stretching exertions of babes,
And the beard's old furrowed ground.

What a kingdom you display
As you call me to delight!
What generosity is mine,
As I survey the infinite world: yours to me.
Here is fruit for all time,
Here is a way picked out with full joy.
Here means without end
Masters a freedom full.

And Death?
Impossible!
And yet:
In Arcadia Ego.

Oh, the break and the bruise;
The tottered reign
Tumbled in dark confusion,
Satanic and shrieking.

Where now the certitudes of joy?
Does Nothing prevail?
Ah, the lie
Given and received.
Must all be broken?
Has wonder fallen to a sum?

Only so the path to Resurrection
When Death has been chewed over,
Met with and faced,
Farmed right through.
But the glory from that encounter braved
What man can tell?

Come, Lord.

I had a pretty pious upbringing, with a mother and a grand-mother who had both tried their vocations as nuns, and an elder sister who became a nun when I was fourteen. There was a chapel in our house with the Blessed Sacrament reserved there, and everyone in the family took prayer as a matter of course, both together as a family and individually alone. My mother would read to us children from an illustrated copy of Butler's *Lives of the Saints* or from the Gospels as often as from fairy stories, and thus the saints and the people of the Gospels were as much a part of our lives as those from the fairy stories. When we went to Horsham, the local town, we would make a visit to the church when we first arrived and put up a candle, and we would always go to Westminster Cathedral immediately on arrival at Victoria Station in London. My grandfather, Hilaire Belloc, was a national Catholic monument, so that all sorts of clerics and others were always in and out of my home; and history and politics and theology, and those who practised them, were a normal part of life.

My continuous memory starts with the Battle of Britain, which was for me such a marvellous event: no fear, just knowing that we would win; and there was my father with a certain air of contented expectancy getting on quietly making Molotov cock-tails to throw at the German tanks, which would soon be coming up the lane. At this time I was taught to know the stars by my aunts and I have never lost their wonder, and the whole business of infinity making me dizzy, and that first grappling with eternity. As a result I and my elder brother would be out each night of that winter of 1940 with a telescope watching the stars and the bombing of London by the Germans, lighting up the northern sky.

Out of that time has come one very significant incident for me. A German bomber was shot down and crashed on to a house about a mile away from my home. I raced over there on my bicycle and arrived before anyone else, and was hoping to get out the machine guns and the belts of ammunition from the wings (for such things gave one great status among the boys in the village). Before I could get very far with this adventure I was stopped by grown-ups, who then appeared, and was told to help collect the bits and tidy the place up. I found a man's hand, torn from its arm, and this has always remained an incredibly important symbol to me of being cut off from the body. A hand is not a hand if it is not joined to an arm; and so with us, if we are cut off from the Body of Christ.

My mother had a very strong telepathy and taught me to take second sight very much for granted. When I was about nine or ten I was standing with my younger brother in the kitchen after breakfast. A strange woman walked between us, and then walked out into the kitchen yard and disappeared. I said, 'Who was that?' He said, 'Who?' for he had not seen her. I left it at that, and did not worry very much: at that age so many things were inexplicable. But later I felt a brooding presence hovering over me and I rushed to my mother in a panic. She simply said, 'That's a ghost: someone has died, and is asking you to pray for her, so we will all go up to the chapel and say a *De profundis*.' So I felt much better, and two days later we had a letter to say that the midwife, who had delivered me and nursed me for the first six months of my life, had died at the moment I saw that apparition walk through the kitchen. It took me many years to rationalize this into a telepathic experience where I projected into visual terms someone thinking of me at that very crucial moment for them. But straight away it made me take visions seriously – they were not things to be ashamed of or suppressed – and it also gave me (through prayer, and recognition of a world beyond this everyday one) a secure means of coping with those elements, which might otherwise overwhelm me.

An incident several years later, when I was seventeen, might be linked with this in my experience: an aeroplane crashed in front of my home and about four or five yards from me, and the two crew members were thrown out at my feet and killed instantly. This was, of course, a fearful shock, but again the thing could be contained by prayer, and I remember my amazement when we called up the local parson and the Catholic parish priest. The parson arrived first, asking, 'Where is the dying man?' and when we said, 'Oh, they are both dead', he replied, 'So there is nothing I can do'. It was extraordinary to me that such a man did not turn to prayer for the dead.

Looking back, with the knowledge of other people's child-hoods, it seems to me that mine was astonishingly secure, ordered to the world about me and to a world beyond the natural.

It was independent and close to elemental things in that we produced most of our own food from pigs and chickens and cows and the garden, drew our own water from the well and had lamps and candles for lights. If we wanted to go on a journey we would as like as not use our own bicycles, even if it meant going a hundred miles. We took it for granted that we would make our own games and amusements, would be taught our own lessons, make our own cider and bottle our own wine. I was secure in the local, rural community, but also in the wider literary community of England, and in the international community of the Catholic Church, at least of Europeans and Americans of every nationality, who were constantly in and out of King's Land to see my grandfather.

My father was a prep school master at the time of my birth in Staffordshire, but when I was about four the family moved to King's Land in Sussex to live with my mother's father, who was in need of being looked after. My father continued teaching, but this now took the form of coaching local boys and girls at home for exams. After my mother had taught me the elements of reading and writing and the catechism and the names of birds and flowers and animals and a vast deal of what, I suppose, would be called folklore and superstition, along with the lives of the saints and how to draw, my father took up more formal schooling, teaching me how to write an essay, Greek, Roman and English History, Geography, French, Latin and Maths. He was a superb teacher and plenty of it remains vividly with me to this day. The whole business of learning was simply and securely bound up with the processes of love, and never seemed a burden or a prison.

In 1942, when I was ten, I was sent to Downside, to the prep school part evacuated from Worth. While I was pretty miserable in those first three years it was never unbearable, and while I was dim compared with my contemporaries, and remained a year behind them all through my eight years of schooling, I was never allowed to feel the least guilt or inadequacy by my parents, and the judgement of no one else mattered very much to me.

In my first summer term an aeroplane crashed on the cricket field at Downside, missing me by about three yards and killing ten boys, one of them my exact contemporary. This made the suddenness of death very real, and added experiential knowledge to an overwhelming preoccupation of my mother's: if we asked whether we were going to the circus next week or if there would be Christmas pudding, or anything else of the future, as like as not she would say quite cheerfully, 'We can't be sure: we may all be dead!' It never struck me that this was particularly morbid, as she made it perfectly clear that death was the gateway to heaven. And so when it did come in her eightieth year that I had to tell her that I wanted to anoint her, as the doctor had said that she would not live beyond the week, her reply was, 'This is the day that I have worked and prayed for all my life.'

The prime personal influence among all my teachers at that time (and many taught me, both in and out of the classroom) was Dom Aelred Watkin, who was ostensibly teaching me Latin and History; it was he who introduced me to the fascination of archaeology and the realities of the medieval world. The former in particular has remained one of the great possessions of my life, giving me a passionate interest in the *things* of the past wherever I am, but it has also sent me further and further back to the origins of mankind, and made me more and more aware of our cultural inheritance, achieved at such cost, and the immense significance and importance of the 'pagan' sense of the numinous and its external physical expression in such things as the megalithic monuments and the later mazes, and so of all the varied and 'irrational' paraphernalia of the Church, like candles and incense and processions and vestments, which so many are destroying without a vestige of an understanding of what they are doing or losing.

Looking back on my time in the school I am amazed now at how little I learned explicitly about prayer, and how ignorant we all were of what went on in the monastery. In my last year I could not make up my mind what to do after leaving, being torn between astronomy, archaeology and boat-building, but as the monks did give the impression of knowing where they were going, and what they were doing, I thought I would like to see what went on in the monastery, and asked to join the novitiate, though I never expected to stay, and did not at the time have any very strong desire to.

I was just eighteen when I entered, and was the youngest of five novices clothed together in 1950, the oldest being sixty-eight, the same age as my father, the other three in their twenties.

The single most important thing I learned was the whole technique of how to pray. I seemed to move incredibly easily into the life of prayer, and I had excellent instructors and guides in my novice master, Dom Alban Brooks, and my confessor, Dom Leander Donovan. Dom Alban was very clear and explicit on how to practise 'recollection'. He would say it was like a door on a spring which would swing back to close once anyone had walked through. So it should be with our hearts and minds: if not actively concerned with some business or person we should 'swing back' to attending to God and to his presence within us and around us. All our work and activity should be done with the awareness of his loving eye, as human lovers just simply revelling in the presence of the beloved. He taught me how to take a formal prayer like the 'Our Father' and to spend half an hour praying each phrase and getting more and more meaning and significance from it. I learned to dwell on a single word like 'love' or 'heaven' or 'beauty', and relate it all to God's creative power and being. We were shown how to build up a 'meditation', picturing some scene from the Gospels in all its visual and audible detail so as to keep the imagination occupied, and then to let the heart and mind dwell on all that could be learned and loved from the incident. We spent much time studying the psalms so as to get more and more spiritual profit from the Office in choir. The music of the plainchant also reinforced this meditative element in so many of the biblical excerpts: the haunting longing to be found in the antiphons of Advent, so often taken from the prophecies of Isaiah; the anguish in Holy Week, dominated by the Lamentations of Jeremiah; the triumph of Easter, expressed in so many of St Paul's exuberant canticles. We learned of the 'Sacrament of the Present Moment' as propounded in Père de Caussade's book *Abandonment to Divine Providence*. We read *The Cloud of Unknowing* with its insistence on setting our hearts upon *desire*. We read the *Revelations of Divine Love* to Julian of Norwich and saw how all shall be well, and all manner of things shall be well. The seeds of all this had been sown in my childhood, but in that first year of the novitiate it came, as it were, into the open, and has ever since provided me with a richness and glory which convince me that, for myself, life would be pretty pointless without it.

Each day there was half an hour of private prayer morning and evening, at least half an hour of spiritual reading in private, as well as half an hour in common aloud with the other novices; there was a low Mass with the novice master, probably another low Mass served, as well as the sung High Mass. Matins and Lauds lasted from 5.20 a.m. till about 6.10; Prime was a short Office at 7.00. Terce was chanted before High Mass, Sext and None at 1.00 p.m. Vespers was from 7.00 till 7.30, Compline at 8.45. In all, this would have amounted to about four hours a day actively taken up with prayer in addition to an hour of spiritual reading – a very powerful and formative experience.

Apart from the whole business of techniques and forms of prayer it was Dom Leander who taught me how to cope with the Abyss and recognize it for what it was. After a period of almost delirious joy in my praying I had an experience of annihilation: I felt that I was being sucked into a 'black hole'. It was a *positive* experience of nothingness. It was the most horrific experience I have ever had: I seemed to be teetering on the edge of becoming nothing. This was not physical, it was not precisely in the mind, it was in the spirit, in the very roots of my being. I went to Dom Leander in a real terror, feeling that at any moment I was going not only out of my mind, but out of existence. And when I told him of it in words of panic and desperation, he replied, 'This is marvellous! This is the best thing that could happen to you; I wish I were there with you in this.' And I said, 'If you can say that, then you have no comprehension of what I am talking about.' He assured me that he did, and that I was experiencing the infinity and total otherness of God. In prayer we keep making concepts or ideas of God, and then making these into God, but as we remain faithful to God, and God to us, he has to break out of everything that appears to contain him, the bottom has to drop out of the world and the effect *appears* to be one of annihilation. It is the best possible foretaste of death. It is the experience of the Passion. It was about this time that I wrote the piece with which this essay opens: 'Wonder is so sudden a gift.'

From that time, while the mode of dying has sometimes appeared frightening, the act of dying has remained for me the great object and goal of living. It has made this life all the more worth living because it is leading me on to an even more fantastic experience. I later found a reference to what I suspect is the same thing in Thornton Wilder's *Ides of March*, but it does not seem to correspond with anything in the regular books on prayer. But then I have never yet found a book setting out to map the whole path of prayer which corresponds all the way with my own experience, and I tend sometimes to agree with one of my fellow novices who said, after about three years in the business, 'The trouble with St John of the Cross is that either one has experienced it all at different times already, or else one hasn't begun at all, and I don't know which is the less likely.'

It is not easy to analyse one's own prayer, and here, almost more than anywhere else, one feels vulnerable at self-revelation, and there is the further danger of limiting one's joys by the act of defining them. But the Venerable Fr Augustine Baker in section iii, chapter vii of *Sancta Sophia* describes a prayer of internal silence which he finds approved in the works of Antonio de Rojas. This appears to me to be the closest to my own present experience.

I set myself to rest in God's presence, not attending to the imagination or verbalizing my attention or intention, except very occasionally; standing empty, if you like, before the fulfilling

Spirit, desiring to be possessed by him; putting all into regard, into desire, into trust. For much of the time this can be hard and daunting, for there is much reassurance to be gained from doing, saying, thinking, imagining specific things. But at other times I am so powerfully aware of the life of the Spirit within me that nothing else I have ever experienced can compare with it. And I worry not about what 'stage' or 'level' I have reached, for I just know that it is good to be here. In 1968 I wrote the following piece for a Sixth Form Society at Downside, called Blue Concrete, when the boys asked me to produce something on the experience of prayer. I meant it to convey something of the process of prayer, and behind the visual and other images it still expresses something important to me.

'HALF-WAY'

The start is numbness,
a gentle unease beyond all grasping.
There is no touch,
even the wind is still
and the warm rain
negative.

Pain would be preferable:
Painfully life can be felt;
it is the first brave assertion,
stepping out from self-engrossed imprisonment.

Over the wall:
what there?
'Nothing', say those who fall back
into the deadening, soft enclosure.

But some scramble over and away
into the fearful unknown,
abandoning the mapmakers' conclusions
exactly arrived at.
For them the brambles
and the rain now lashing cold;
hunger and fear in the darkness,
but somehow company and a direction,
if only outwards
from that dead centre.

And I am there
suddenly in the midst of them.

What now?
Where are the points of reference?

Will there be eating or sleeping on the way?
Is this dark depth pregnant with new world?
    Who can tell:
    Let us accept direction with agnosticism.

But I:
I am taken;
taken by the hand,
a hand rough from the hard work of discovery
and the thing achieved.

There is possibility.

Heights rear up
and the demand intolerable.
Up that sheer side?
Faith in so frail a thread?
Think what can now be lost!
Can I not hoard my scrupulous treasures,
picked up along a swift road's passage?
And settle
for no more possibility?

No:
Once more up and away
and the few lights' delight
soon lost.
Mist now,
and the ever crushing weight
of sheer height
achieved at rasping cost:
the air asserts its brutal ascendency.
Breath becomes all.
And yet,
And yet,
beyond breath
is the ascent, still calling.
The mist thinning and receding.
Can there be view?
Can there be vision?
Arrival?
Richness given and received?

Achievement is possibility:
Meeting is imminent.

9

And, dear God,
—still going—
I am glad I went.

The novitiate started, or gave an impetus to, a lot of other processes: I grew five inches in that period and first began really to develop intellectually. In the school it had been a fearful effort to cope with work set or to understand what people were talking about, but now that started to fall into place and I began to get immense joy and satisfaction out of intellectual pursuits. Dom Aelred introduced me to the early writings of the Fathers of the Church and to Migne's atrocious print and the marvellous folios of the Maurists. Incredible though it may sound, although I had done Classics through to Sixth Form in the school, I had never just sat down with a Latin or a Greek book and simply read it. Always there was the business of construing, looking up all the references, noting parallels and the rest, but within a week of entering the novitiate I was given St Augustine's commentary on the psalms, all 400 folio pages of it to read, and so did I learn to read Latin without any effort of translating as I went along. That was followed by his commentary on St John, then St Leo's *Tome*, and for the next ten years my room was never free from some book of the Fathers. It was all an immensely formative experience for me, giving me yet another insight into origins (this time of the Church) and teaching me how growth is a slow and sometimes seemingly unsteady thing, and how vast is the area of knowledge in any field, and how staggering can be people's arrogance in the face of their stupefying ignorance. How marvellous are the riches preserved for us in the Fathers, and how appalling it is that a generation of monks and priests is now arriving who think that they have lost nothing by throwing over the inheritance of Latin and Greek. As soon claim to understand India or China, having seen a film about them on television.

Next the novitiate taught me that there is no marvellous secure state when one will be 'grown-up' and everything will be clear and simple. From an early stage people were coming to pour out their troubles and difficulties and expecting me to help. For a long time I resented this, and could not understand why it happened, but eventually I got to see that if the Lord God had given me a nice face that people felt they could confide in, this could be as good a way as any of doing his will, and I began to see that while it is a splendid thing to be as solid and stable as a rock, the really fantastic thing is life with its balance of unstable forces like a hovering bird, and that the life of the mind and spirit are more exciting still. Finally there was the love and intensive interaction and joy of one's fellow novices in that tight little community largely cut off even from the rest of the monastic community. It was full of laughter and the shared experience of exploration, and Downside seemed to me (as it still does) to be the most marvellous group of men to belong to in the world, with the possible exception of the Twelve Apostles.

I said earlier that I entered the novitiate out of a certain sense of curiosity, and never really expected to stay, and many people find that surprising when I say it, but for myself I am amazed at the numer who apparently enter a novitiate with their minds already made up. How *can* they be so sure? For me things went very easily from September until December and the end of the school term, but when all the boys left for home, and my younger brother with them, I felt desperately homesick. Soon afterwards all sorts of things seemed to be getting difficult and I can remember kneeling in choir in the dark saying my prayers and thinking, 'If only I wasn't *here*, if I was in any other situation in the world, everything would be fine.' Then I had a blinding revelation of just how ridiculous that was, and I suspect that this was a turning point, though it only became clear to me in the spring that followed, when I was looking east from my cell window on the top floor towards Salisbury Plain and my beloved Sussex beyond. I was longing to visit Shipley again, to talk to everyone in the village, to see where the coots and moorhens were nesting on the lake, to see what the woodsmen had been doing to the trees, to talk to the bulls on the farm and to find the first blackbird's nest or a robin's. But I suddenly realized that I wanted to see all that, and then come back: my centre of gravity had changed. And from that moment I have never had a single doubt about where I should be.

This brings me to another of the incredible gifts showered upon me. My home was in the shadow of a great windmill—the tallest in Sussex and still working—and this was a sign and symbol to me of all the goodness and glory in my home and upbringing. When as children we were returning from a long journey we would be looking for the Mill and would vie with each other to be the first to see her, and how my heart lifted whenever she came into view, or when she peeped over the Wealden Forest when one got on to higher ground and looked back.

When I left King's Land for the novitiate at Downside I thought that if I did stay I would lose that intense joy of home and the complete sense of belonging, and that when I did return for a visit or a holiday it would be as a guest, as someone from outside. But it has not been so: I did not lose that centre and bedrock of my life, I simply gained another, so that now my heart leaps when I see the Abbey tower over the hills as much as when I see the Mill. It has been nothing but gain. It is the same with the community: for all the ups and downs and pressures and frictions which can occur, I really do enjoy being with every single member of the community, as I also do with my own brothers and sister. I am in the happy state of not being able to imagine a greater fundamental fulfilment than I have been given.

It was the sight of the Mill, when I was walking alone, aged about seventeen, and when I came out of Green Street Gorse and saw her suddenly (though not unexpectedly) below me, with Chanctonbury and the Downs beyond, that caught me up in the first of my ecstasies, a glory beyond words or anything I had previously experienced. I was inebriated, exalted, totally free of all limitation or restraint, at one with the whole incredible adventure of living. It came without any warning, as suddenly as a gap in the clouds when one is walking in the hills; it took me outside time, outside the ordinary joys of sense or intellect, it came as a gift, and I thanked God as the giver. I did not talk about it to anyone at the time, and it was only much later that I came across accounts of similar experiences, notably in my grandfather's *Path to Rome*, where he describes his 'Vision of the Alps', and in Richard Jefferies's *The Story of My Heart*. Later still I was to find Marghanita Laski's book *Ecstasy* very illuminating on the subject and to recognize the distinctions between 'nature' ecstasies and 'religious'. These have been the most important experiences in my life, for I believe them to be the nearest we can get on earth to the reality of heaven – what Bishop Bossuet called 'an eternal gasp of wonder'.

I know the pundits on prayer tend to discount such experiences and say that we should not pray in order to get them, and I suppose there is a truth in that. But I only know that God loves me because of his gifts to me. And it is a poor sort of response to a gift not to rejoice in it. And if joy is not the object of life, I do not know what is. And if you are always looking for the dangers and pitfalls you will never see the view, and your life will be the poorer for it, and if you try to skate without falling over you will never know what skating really means. But for myself I really believe that God loves me, and is constantly thinking up new ways to bring me joy, as is the way of all true lovers. So if this is the way to hell then it has been a pretty glorious one.

After my year as a novice things began to take shape and quicken up for me intellectually, and Dom Illtyd Trethowan introduced me to the ordered mind of philosophy and taught me to think theologically. This opened out an immense field of excitement in which I have never ceased to glory. For a time I thought I could be a scholar, and could achieve great things at the creative level, and it took me a long time to learn the lessons of my own limitations in this area. I drove myself so hard that I had a breakdown which took the form of throbbing pains in the head, the inability to sleep for more than half an hour at any one time, going blind if I read or wrote for more than two hours, and acute and frequent migraines. For four months I suffered this with a great sense of frustration and grievance. Why should this have happened to me? Why had God taken away the only things in life that seemed to matter? How could I go on bearing this continuous and acute pain and the sleepless nights? Why could the doctors do nothing about it and simply say it would get right in the end, not knowing when?

And then this extraordinary gift was given to me: it came out of an empty sky, as it were, without my noticing, like the dark night moving towards the dawn. There came a day when I was able to recognize that *this* was the way God was loving me at the moment and that all the pain and fear and limitation were as much his gift as the previous joy and fulfilment, that it was like being hugged very close to your mother's breast: difficult to breathe, and you can't see anything, but yet it is love. And with that I was set free: the pain and sleeplessness and the blindness went on for another five years, but they were as irrelevant to my fundamental well-being as the soaking one gets when sailing, or the knocks in a game of rugger. Indeed I was free among the dead (as the psalmist says) and seem ever to have remained so in the depths of my spirit, whatever may be the ruffling up of the surface.

I wrote several prayers at this time, and perhaps it is worth reproducing two of them here to point to what I was experiencing.

> Lord, I confess that you are good, and that to you all gentleness and love belong. And when there comes upon me the great pain of my heart and head, it is to you that I must look, and the look must be one of love, not reproach. If any should be reproachful it is you, who have stretched out your hands all the day and I would not . . .

> O Lord my God, I stand upright when I should bow and kneel: how else can I learn but through the humbling discipline of pain – and that (at first) the least of pains, which is in the body.

> Let me not forget that pain is our work, and is the token which has

the power of being honoured in much gold. You have said that those you love you chastise. Can it be that you love me? That cannot be – and yet, it must be, for yours is the true love, which stretches forth its hands all the day.

Do you remember when I longed for death, and thought to be, in one brief hour, with you in Paradise? And do you remember how that changed, and how I saw that I was standing penniless before your door? And how in fear I prayed for life?

What now? Life is a pain indeed, but it makes for Death. Still am I penniless. But you are rich, and you and I (but how, O God? Oh, to see that mystery!) you and I are one.

But if you and I are one, then my pain is your pain, and since the pain is your love, why then, it is my love. And if I have your love when I feel your pain, then surely have I overcome the world.

Lord, I am a poor fool: teach me the Wisdom which played before the eternal hills. Teach me the Wisdom which is Love divine, and give me the Trust which brings your Peace.

O Lord, show me gratitude, for I am yours.

But some of my prayers were not so desperate:

Dear Lord, my Lord, my all, make me to want, to want to need ever and ever so much more. Was there fatigue? Let the nights come longer. Hunger and thirst? Let food and drink be withheld. Longing for love and companionship? Let there be rejection and forgetfulness – so be the longing, the desire, the want be increased; the *capacity* grow beyond limit.

A chance to give? The power to be generous? Yes: and a thousand times more.

I have so little time, so little space.
Take from me, that I may give.
Open wide that wound to let your Spirit in.
I must watch, I must wait, I must need, I must beg.

You live in the darkness. So be it.
Ah, grant me but this: that I stand in want
Till that want is so wide that only you can fill it.
Keep me from safe, warm acquiescence. Give me urgency and the
ranging spirit.

Take all, that I may be all for you, that all from me
may mean all from you, all for you.
May you be my all
in all.

Only your strength, your vision, your command,
your wilderness.
Mine to follow after.
O God, *quam terribilis es.*
I fear, even as I say it, but I confess
I hold
I affirm.
> *Quod scripsi*
> *scripsi.*

It was at this time also that there was another aeroplane crash very near me, killing more people, and there was a great fire at Downside during which I was sent several times into a blazing building to do rescue work, which I found very frightening. As a result I began to have a series of nightmares, particularly of my bedroom being on fire, and several times in my sleep I jumped out of the window as the only way to escape. My bedroom was on the ground floor at the time, so I came to no real harm, but later I had to sleep two, and then three floors up, and it was a sobering and excellent thing for me having to face as a present reality that there was a fair chance that I would jump to my death before morning. This was a very effective way of keeping active in me St Benedict's injunction in the fourth chapter of the Rule to keep death daily before one's eyes. I have never had any difficulty in desiring eternal life with a spiritual desire, as he commands us in the same chapter. So I hope that when death does come I will meet him with open eyes, and at the very top of my form.

In 1967 I was told that my dear friend, Siegfried Sassoon, was dying of cancer in a hospital in Warminster, and the next day I rode the twenty-five miles on a bicycle to see him. When I went into the room the disease had got so fierce a grip on him that I thought for a moment he was already dead: his neck seemed no thicker than my arm, his cheeks and eyes sunk into great hollows. But then he opened his eyes, and gave that great smile of his and said that he knew I would come to see him before he went. We talked of Belloc and of his influence in bringing Siegfried into the Church, of how Kent was doing in the county cricket, of his own cricket with the Downside Ravens and of our very different boyhoods in the Weald. Then he said, 'I am sorry not to be in better form', and I replied that I thought him in fine form, and he said, 'Yes, underneath this little heap of a body I am at the very top of my form, and is it wrong to be looking forward to being in Paradise this week?' I said he must do just that thing, and then urged him to go home to Heytesbury to die in his own bed and not be bullied by all the medical people. And so I left him, and he went to heaven two days later, and as I biked home through the woods of Longleat I thought how of all the many deaths I had seen, in spite of my complete conviction of the resurrection, this was the first I had come away from – not that I actually saw him die – with a sense of enlargement: in all the other cases death has seemed to take something from me, to leave me somehow less alive. And I suppose this is right and unavoidable, for *Mors et Vita duello conflixere mirando* ('Death and Life are caught up in a wonderful conflict'). But life should also have its say when it reaches to true holiness. So, at a later date, when I came to anoint before his death my own father, who was the holiest man I have ever known, I felt the same sense of being enlivened as he said, 'Oh, what a marvellous life I have had!'

Another crucial moment of my life was my ordination to the priesthood. As I have already said, it soon became clear to me that I should become a monk, and this I came very much to desire, but I did not want to be a priest, for it seemed to me to be a fearful responsibility to be God's representative in this way, and to be dispensing the sacraments and preaching his word and guiding the penitent. But at that time, before the Second Vatican Council, it was a requirement of Canon Law that all choir monks be priests, so I accepted it as one of the conditions of my remaining at Downside as a monk. When it came to my solemn profession, I took my vows with firm conviction and satisfaction but with no spiritual uplift or sensible joy: it was about as *emotionally* significant as eating breakfast. But on the day of my ordination, the Archdeacon called me out, and I answered '*Adsum*', and then I lay on my face before the altar as the Bishop and my whole community sang the litany of the saints, calling for God's grace to support me, and I was given one of the great spiritual experiences of my life. I felt almost physically lifted up and carried by those prayers and by the presence of the whole communion of saints, and then I realized that it was not *I* who had to take all that responsibility, but that it was our Lord dwelling in me who would be working through me: 'You did not choose me, but I chose you and appointed you that you should go and bear fruit and that your fruit should abide' (John 15.16 RSV). That conviction of Christ's indwelling has never left me through all the panics and inadequacies and failures that seem to be an inevitable accompaniment of any achievement on this earth. I remembered what my grandfather once wrote on the portrait of a child in his book *On Something*: 'Blessedness and Sacredness and Holiness are bound together in one, but of these three Sacredness is your chief business. Sacredness, which is the mark of that purpose whose air is blessedness, whose end is holiness, will be upon you till you die; maintain it and let it be your chief concern.' And I have never had to go back on that prayer of King David which I had printed on my ordination card:

> Domine Deus, in simplicitate cordis mei laetus obtuli universa; et populum tuum, qui repertus est, vidi cum ingenti gaudio: Deus Israel, custodi hanc voluntatem.

> Lord God, in the simplicity of my heart I joyfully offer you the whole universe; and your people who have been found I look upon with great joy: O God of Israel, keep this my intention.

(1 *Paralipomenon* 29.17)

After my ordination I was sent to Worth for a year and had my first experience of teaching, and I learned a great deal about my inadequacies as a communicator and an inspirer. The classroom is a great preparation for the pulpit. In the classroom they come back at you, so that you have to justify what you have said, but also having 'taught' the class something you learn from the correction of the exercise how little has got across. Then I remember an occasion when I was going through with a boy of about ten an extra piece of Latin that he had done of his own accord because he was behind the rest and wanted to catch up. I said, 'That's wrong. This should have been in the accusative. Have you already forgotten what I told you about the subjunctive? There, you still haven't learned the Latin for a horseman . . .' Then, as I was getting to the end of the sentences, finding fault with every single one, he stood up, hit me hard in the stomach and ran off. He taught me far more about appreciating the good in what people have done than I fear I ever taught him Latin.

From Worth I was sent up to Cambridge to read for a degree in Classics. As so often in my life, I did not choose this or want it, but accepting it from God I found it marvellous and I enjoyed it to the full. It gave me the opportunity to read Greek classical literature pretty well from end to end, from Homer to Aristotle, and that is an incredible gift to be given. Those writings have been a possession for ever in epic, lyric, tragedy, history and philosophy. Because I was already embedded in the Fathers of the Church and the vast medieval achievement I was less excited by classical Latin literature, except for Vergil, Catullus, Propertius and Tacitus. But throughout it all I was finding the despair amid the pagan splendour. I was living before the resurrection: it made me realize the grandeur and the frailty of the human spirit and let me catch something of the incredible impact of Christianity when it came fresh upon the world. What a mature thing Christianity is, how it needs the great pagan sense of awe, slow building and the absoluteness of the grave, before the new life of Christ can be appreciated. Sophocles could get the chorus in his play *Antigone* to say: 'There are many wonders in the world, but none has arisen more wonderful than Man . . . He has learned the use of language, thought as quick as the wind . . . There is nothing beyond his ingenuity. He can come to every chance prepared. He has found a remedy for every ill, *save only Death*.'

The bedrock of the Classics has made me feel at home in all subsequent European literature. This was another great linking-up of continuities. It helped me to write myself, both prose and verse. I came to understand what the Greeks meant by the Muse, and I have tried to be faithful to her when she comes so unexpectedly, or after long and painful search.

I revelled in all this time and gave myself to a great many people and things besides the Classics with a good deal of abandon, largely, I think, because I knew it was going to end after three years, and I had no desire that it should continue longer. My headaches and sleeplessness continued through it all, and when it came to the exams, if they were three-hour papers, I had to get them finished in two hours, as after that the blindness came down. At least it taught me to work fast and to trust to inspiration, so that I got a degree largely because I did not worry about whether I got one or not. The important thing was studying the literature, not passing the exam.

In the summer vacation from Cambridge I tried to get pastoral experience and for two years I supplied at Beccles in Suffolk to enable the parish priest to take a holiday. This was an immensely illuminating experience, because I found for the first time in my life that I was in a position of authority and responsibility and was expected to give advice, make decisions, teach, comfort and direct people far older, wiser and better than myself. But everybody welcomed me, talked to me in the street, listened respectfully to what I said and generally made it clear that I was the next best thing to God in Beccles. It made me realize how very important is community life, where the brethren quickly and cheerfully tell you where you have gone wrong and how to improve matters. The apparent adulation and total acceptance of everything I said and did in the parish was pleasant for a week or so, but it was no way that I could live a whole life.

In my third long vacation I worked in a small parish in the centre of Liverpool: St Mary's, Highfield Street. I will never forget being sent to visit the great Eye Hospital. I went into the first ward, and said to the Sister, 'I am the new Catholic chaplain. Could you please tell me who are the Catholics in this ward?' 'I will certainly not tell you,' she replied. 'You are a priest: you should visit everybody in the ward.' She was right: one's priesthood is God's gift for all mankind.

From that day on I cannot count the number of occasions when I have been approached by, or allowed to approach, people in every sort of need because I was recognized as a priest. I cannot agree with those priests who say they do not wear clerical dress because it puts up a barrier between them and other people. It may possibly put up a barrier sometimes, but I believe that far more often it is an opening and a reassurance.

In 1960 I came down from Cambridge to teach in the school and to be a curate in Midsomer Norton. In 1962 I was made a housemaster. For the last twenty years life has been one long hectic rush, and it seems more difficult to pick out much of a pattern of progress or illumination, though I have felt God's hand in so many things. It has become harder and harder to find time to pray, to read, to think. Sleep has been less broken, but in term time at least I have seldom been getting more than five or six hours in bed. I have been preparing classes on the way to the classroom, writing difficult letters of spiritual direction or comfort sentence by sentence between the telephone calls and the knocks at the door, and missing meals for up to twenty-four hours at a stretch because of people arriving with desperate personal crises; I have been preparing sermons and conferences on the way to the church or even on the way up to the pulpit.

For as a housemaster you are acting as mother and father to seventy boys away from home, sometimes 10,000 miles from home. You are encouraging them, protecting them, rebuking them, advising them; in fact taking to heart and trying to put into practice all that St Paul felt for his beloved churches. When you have been on the move for eighteen hours and have had only a cup of coffee since a hurried supper the day before, the telephone rings and a parent in Hong Kong says cheerfully, 'Good morning, Father!'

In my first two years as a housemaster, teacher of Latin, Greek and Religious Instruction, school librarian, fencing master and secretary to the Abbot's council, there were times when I did not much care whether I lived or died. What undoubtedly kept me sane – if I did keep sane – was the unfailing support of the community, especially Dom Aelred the headmaster and Dom Raphael Appleby, my nextdoor neighbour as a housemaster and appointed on the same day as myself. Also, the daily round of public and private prayer, bringing stillness to the day at its beginning and end, kept me on course.

But sometimes when I felt desperate I would go out on my bicycle to some abandoned quarry on Mendip and start climbing up the rough sheer face. When I was forty or fifty feet up it would begin to get frightening, for a fall would probably mean death, and I had no rock-climbing equipment or protective clothing, and I would begin to want to live again. Then, when I had completed the climb and lay physically exhausted and emotionally drained on the top of the cliff, I could go home with the sense that life felt very positive again. It was an irresponsible thing to do and I cannot now justify it. Now I do not need such desperate remedies, though they seemed to help at the time.

On one occasion I had got on to a narrow ledge forty feet up and could not reach any satisfactory handhold above. I found it impossible to go back the way I had come up, and then the ledge on which I was standing began to crumble. As it finally fell away beneath my feet I jumped sideways and upwards to the hold which I had just decided was out of reach. This taught me a great lesson: you often will not get an ability or the energy until you really need it. But when you *must* do a thing, then you can. I doubt whether this is good advice to rock-climbers, but I have found it to have a great many other applications in the course of my life. And one thing that seems to have happened literally dozens of times is that when I feel at my last gasp, at the end of a frightful day, and am desperately trying to comfort someone on the phone, or when I have given a disaster of a sermon or a class because I have been too pressed by other things, when nothing has signified or carried conviction to me as I said it – these are the occasions when I am more often than not told that I have said just the right thing, that I have changed the person's life, that I must have put a lot of hard work and prayer into that sermon to have hit it off so perfectly . . . And of course the explanation is that at times like these I have ceased to have the pride and self-sufficiency to get in the way of the Spirit's own action. True inspiration has followed.

Some years ago I was asked to preach on prayer to a large Methodist congregation and I did not know how to start, what was the common ground between us, whether I would sound banal or completely beyond them. I talked it over with Dom Raphael, who said, Don't worry: don't talk to them *about* prayer, just trust in the Spirit and get them to pray. I was absolutely terrified, but I went without any notes and nothing formally prepared. I got into the pulpit and said I was going to call on the Spirit to pray in us all. I verbalized some of it, much of it was in silence, and I have never had so many people come to me after a sermon or service to say that it had really changed their lives more than any other religious experience. The effect was palpable.

I trust explicitly to this inspiration and guidance increasingly, and in my clearer moments I wonder why I ever hold back. But the temptation to be self-sufficent can still return, the failure to trust absolutely to the all-embracing love of our dear Lord.

Human frailty is a great mystery, especially my own. But at least it teaches me to be more patient with others in their manifest inadequacies and to go on living and working with them, since I still go on living with my own inadequate self and cheerfully call on the Lord to take over when I have got myself into some impossible jam. I always need to remember the parallel between the community and the individual member of it. I think it of crucial importance that we carry in ourselves the marks of Christ crucified, and the whole agony of the divisions, frustrations, fears and emptinesses of our communities and of the whole Church. Pope Paul VI was a vivid and visible example of a man so crucified, but one who by that very suffering not only held the Church together, but gave it Christ's life. We are called in our communities to that same witness.

I also learned something important to me about human frailty through fasting. There is very little physical austerity at Downside and what little fasting was expected of us in the novitiate and afterwards seemed completely pointless. It was not sharp enough to hurt, and anyway what was achieved by giving oneself a headache by abstaining from food that was available? How can it please God simply to hurt ourselves? But there is a very strong tradition in both the Old and New Testaments, exemplified by John the Baptist, Jesus and many, many monks and holy men after them, witnessing to the importance of fasting. It was not until I made the pilgrimage to Lough Derg in Ireland that I got some idea of its significance. During this three-day pilgrimage you have but one meal in the day and that of dry oatmeal biscuits and hot water. On the last day I was there I did not even get that, so in the end I went without food or drink of any kind for forty-eight hours and the previous forty-eight had been sustained only by a handful of dry biscuits. It taught me a lot. First I found how savagely dependent I am on the wealth of my circumstances: how after twenty-four hours' fasting my belly is the centre of my consciousness; how I can do *nothing* without food and, therefore, without the love of God who provides it. I know of few more effective ways of cutting down one's sense of independence, pride and self-sufficiency. Next, it gives one a new sense of the incredible significance and interdependence of this material universe and of my little body in particular. Furthermore, as you continue with it you get a clarity of spiritual perception, you leave behind another whole dimension of concern. You are given a new freedom. I think our monastic fathers were right to underline its importance and I do not intend to let it cease to be a part of my life.

Another part of the monastic tradition which I could not really understand and which I long wanted to experience, was the 'desert'. In its literal sense it was beyond my reach in England, yet all the old monks took its importance for granted and I was convinced that you could not understand whole layers of meaning in the Bible and in the monastic tradition unless you had experienced the 'desert'.

In August 1977 I had my chance. I had been sent out to Australia by the Abbot in response to an invitation from Sydney University to be the representative of Downside and to give a paper at a conference on the centenary of the death of Bede Polding, first Archbishop of Sydney and a monk of Downside. On the way home I spent five days in Israel, staying with some Israeli friends in Jerusalem. I wanted to drive to Mount Sinai, but it was the hottest week ever recorded in Jerusalem and I was told that quite simply I would die if I tried to go to Sinai. But I did get to the Dead Sea and then off alone into the Wilderness of Judaea, and it had a most profound effect upon me.

All the cares, multiplicities and busyness of the world almost instantly fell away from me as I walked up that stark and lonely wadi in the blazing heat of the afternoon. The silence enveloped me like a blanket. This caught me completely by surprise, but it should have been obvious: noise comes from men and machines, animals, water and wind in the trees. None of these are in the desert except the wind and that has to blow hard against the rocks to make any noise. I quickly realized how days and nights of this could teach one many things and I saw at once why the prophets and the monks retreated here to find God imperious in this solitude of no irrelevancies. In such a terrain and condition there can be no way of escaping the fixed majestic questioning of the Spirit. The sun is an enemy who threatens your life and your sanity. It seems alive and nothing else is living, except snakes and other small animals that live in holes in the ground and come out at night.

My time alone in the desert was far too short, but I count it the most significant single experience of my journey round the world. Later I wrote this of it:

The Desert is silent.
Why was this unexpected?
Only the wind can call
where no life is,
and water fled.
Ravens high searching for carrion
give rare and distant voice,
but the still rocks speak no word
as they shimmer in the heat.
And yet the soul is summoned forth
to give answer clear enough
as the Sun's pitiless eye,
veiled by no cloud of the softly irrelevant,
sees straight to the ultimate question:
Whence is your being?
Who is your Master now?
The beasts of the Desert
are creatures of the night perforce.
For here the Moon is the only friend:
I saw her rise full
between the misty mountains,
drawing her silvery path
over the sulphurous waters
of that deepest desert
wherein the Jordan dies.

My life was turned:
I passed right through:
My tent is left behind.

Since that time I have come to realize that God can call us into a desert of his own making and choosing, whatever our circumstances, and that the essential elements of this have been with me for a long time: the sense of not being in control of one's surroundings, of being called beyond one's apparent capacities and defences. But for all that, I am immensely grateful for having been allowed to feel the heat of that furnace which has forged so much of three of the world's great religions.

I suppose that all this furious activity of the past twenty years, first as a housemaster for thirteen years, then as deputy headmaster for five, and now as headmaster of 600 boys and eighty teaching staff, seems far removed from the conventional ideas of the peace and quiet of the cloister. In my first six months as headmaster I have made journeys to London several times, and also to Edinburgh, Dublin, Oxford, Cambridge, Lourdes, Exeter, Sussex, Dorset and Shropshire, besides dozens of shorter trips in the vicinity. I attended meetings, gave papers, preached, prayed in public, listened to other people or just sat and looked at the view. I have been dictating twenty to thirty letters a day, teaching Latin and Political Theory to the Fifth and Sixth Forms, chairing meetings of housemasters, heads of Faculties, parents, Old Boys, prefects. In snatched moments I have been writing my contribution to this book and reading and making suggestions about the other parts, as well as chairing meetings to discuss them. I have given long interviews to the press and television.

My day starts at 5.00 a.m. with the Office of Matins recited privately, followed by thirty minutes of mental prayer and my private Mass. This is really the only part of the day when I can be virtually certain of no interruption and I therefore reserve it for that most important element of my life. By 6.30 I am dictating letters on to a tape or preparing papers for use later in the day. I have little chance of getting to any of the monastic offices in the church, but will make a real effort to share at least one meal or period of recreation with my brethren each day when I am at Downside. I am hardly ever in bed before 11.00 p.m., and usually it is closer to midnight. My last hour or so of the day is again spent in prayer and meditation or reading.

There is a definite temptation to put off for the time being the fulfilment of the vow of *Conversio Morum*, to get simply carried along by the tide of activity and to leave until retirement the pursuit of monastic perfection. Then as I return quietly to my desired haven in the archivist's office, I shall be able to attend to the things of God, spend more time and energy on prayer, prayerful reading, meditation, preaching and writing . . . For me this is a romantic dream and the denial and rejection of all that God has been ceaselessly showering upon me throughout this glorious experience of life he has given me.

I believe that in their essentials and in a lot of their details, the circumstances of my present life are those positively willed by God (some of them, of course, are the result of my own errors) and that in this great whirlwind of activity and distraction is to be found my Desert, my calling. I can find plenty of examples of monks from St Gregory the Great to John Bede Polding to encourage me in the belief that sanctity can be found in the mess I am *now* in, rather than in the chimera of tomorrow's imagined peace.

24

God still speaks to me in the quiet of my prayer, in the love and support of my monastic brethren and my family, in the generosity and patience of boys and staff, in the courage and concern of parents and Old Boys, in the love and joy of so many friendships made and maintained down the years. I still find him in the stars at night, in a spring wood, in the vision of the great poets and the prophets, both past and present.

In all of this and in still more that I could not or would not list, I am constantly called to transcend the confines of my little world, but also to go deeper into the mystery of my own being, which I believe lives only because Christ lives in me.

Someone who read this piece asked me how I differed from the boy of forty years ago and the novice of thirty years ago. At the time I almost wholly failed to give a proper answer, having never thought about the question. But I think it a very valid one to ask and on reflection I would say this of myself:

It is important not to lose our childhood, as Jesus insists, and in many ways I do not think I have lost mine. I still feel the security and assurance of love around me, from my natural family, from my community and from God. I continue to live among people who regard prayer as something as normal and natural as eating and drinking. I still find the bridges from this life to the everlasting round every corner, but the glory of this natural life is still, in itself, justification enough for existence: in the most fundamental way I have no worries or cares about the life I have been given (and I do feel it is given rather than made by me) in spite of all the day-to-day frustrations, doubts and fears with which I am assailed. I feel at home in the universe.

How then have I changed? In a lot of ways I do not find people or things so simple or so clearly right or wrong: I find it much more difficult to judge. I have now also got a great deal of intellectual paraphernalia and rejoice in the satisfactions of argument, discussion and oratory. I have lost the very strong shyness of my childhood (Cambridge did that for me) and now I basically regard strangers as potential friends rather than as threats. But with this developing extrovert side of my character I have not lost a very powerful, secret life within, shared with none but God. This, I think, makes me more self-sufficient than the majority of people I know at all well. I realize increasingly the overwhelming importance of the second half of life, when one's natural powers are waning and making way for the complete takeover by the Spirit. Increasingly I see death not as an escape or release from this life, but as the greatest, as well as the culminating, experience. But at the same time I am far more aware of the tremendous significance of the eternal choice for life or death awaiting me. I am also more and more aware, as a fact of experience, that I can achieve nothing on my own and that all must be attributed to God and his overall providence. I have always rejoiced in life in all its manifestations, but I am increasingly explicit in my reverence for all its forms and can no longer justify killing anything except for the furtherance of life in other ways. I am very conscious of the unity of all life – the vision of Teilhard de Chardin has had a great effect on me in this respect – and of the interdependence of its different manifestations: that the life of one thing can only be maintained at the cost of another's death. I see all life as coming from God, as his messenger, and returning to him. I see more clearly the reality of St Paul's appeal to the witness of the life of Christ within us. This is the foundation of my joy.

Dear Lord, how you take me: what great messages you hold for me: kept through the ages of ages and then laid out for me. And yet this is but a glimpse and a flicker of what you are and what you hold in store.

Oh, how the light was with us last night as the sun went down: what depth and gradation and everlasting vaulting all across the skies, and trees lambent at the dark edges, filled with the thrushes' first song to spring's adventure.

I could not walk tiptoe enough as you bore me through that rain-washed air, smelling the year's turning and all life's awakening. The wind, so gentle on my cheeks, was drawing, drawing the high cirrus traceries across that unimaginable sky.

Gently, how gently, did you enter me, by all my doors laid open. Grant it now to me that this, through me, may be for all.

I am: I am fed: I am free.

Here is blessing.

A Tapestry, from the Wrong Side

DAME MARIA BOULDING

When I was about sixteen I realized that I had to be a nun. This realization was, in psychological terms, a very ordinary, matter-of-fact event; I was not even praying at the time, but just looking out of a window. There was no sudden flash; it was rather as though the truth had been there in my mind for a long time, but I had only just turned to look directly at it and recognized consciously that it was there – as when you are in a room with another person but are not looking at him, and then at some moment you turn and look. I did not have, either then or subsequently, any extraordinary spiritual experience. I have indeed come to believe that each one of us is specially chosen, loved and called by God, but I also believe that experience of God can come through events that are part of the weave of our ordinary lives. At the time of which I am speaking there was no sense of discontinuity; rather, a simple, quiet feeling that I couldn't do anything else. I don't mean that there was any kind of compulsion or any conviction that I wouldn't be able to make a success of marriage or a career. It was just that if I was going to be the real me, the choice was already made.

I was also immediately aware that I would have to look for some form of contemplative life. It was difficult to explain this choice, especially to other people, but a vital element in it was the mystery of the Church as Christ's Body. There were so many things I wanted to do or be, so many worthwhile ways of living and loving. But if it is true that we are all organically linked together within the life of Christ, all sharing in the one circulation, then any fruitful activity by any member of Christ is done in the power of that life and belongs to us all. I could understand enough to see that a dedicated life at the heart of this Body therefore contributes in some unseen way to the vigour and fertility of the whole; and I somehow knew that contemplatives were there, involved at the hidden centre. This intuition is still of primary importance to me.

I did not know any contemplative nuns, but I read what I could get hold of about some of the main traditions. The breadth and simplicity of Benedictine spirituality attracted me and I was already fairly familiar with the history of the Benedictines. I remember looking through *The Catholic Directory* to find out where there were any live ones, before making contact with Stanbrook.

In September 1947 I entered the Stanbrook novitiate, full of the stark simplicities and radical views of eighteen. It was all quite clear: one wanted the absolute and was impatient to get on with it. I was pretty disconcerted to find how ordinary and human it all was; I remember even being slightly shocked that someone had made up the bed. In the months that followed there was a lot of kindness and new interests and I was happy. This very fact was the occasion of the first temptation: monastic life wasn't hard enough, there was too much of a bump down into the ordinary. Something would elude me if this was all there was to it. It was like the disillusionment after marriage, I suppose. I was tempted to leave and look for a more austere way of life. The temptation evaporated fairly soon, because the spiritual demands of the life on which I had entered became progressively clearer.

By the time I was in temporary vows a little more self-know-ledge had come: a little more recognition of my own weakness and some experience of the desert within. From this came a much more severe temptation, almost the opposite of the earlier one: I thought I couldn't face lifelong commitment to I knew not what. It was terrifyingly open-ended and I had very cold feet at the prospect of solemn profession. I wanted to leave, yet at the same time I knew that there was nothing to go to, in the sense that if I ran away, life would not be real and I would never find what I was seeking. It went on for a long time and there seemed to be no answer. Then one day it simply dropped away. I remember the moment clearly; again, I wasn't even praying. I was gloomily eating my dinner at second table after serving or reading at the community meal, when something very quiet and simple happened; it was as though the fear and worry dropped gently away, now that I had had plenty of time to get the message about my inability to cope alone. I knew that the Lord himself would bear the responsibility with me. It was gentle and deflating and left me wondering what all the fuss had been about. So in due course I took solemn vows and knew it was right. At least, I knew for the time being.

Meanwhile, a perspective of understanding had been given to me: I understood my vocation in terms of the cross and resurrection, the paschal mystery of Christ. It seemed as though this theme had been stamped upon my life from the first. I had been born in paschal time; I received the monastic habit in Easter week; I made my simple vows in Easter week the following year; then three years later my solemn profession was in Easter week. The themes and Scripture texts, the atmosphere and mystery of Holy Week and Easter, had become inextricably mixed up with my vocation: with the fundamental inspiration of it and my grappling to understand. This has been a constant, ever since.

The early years after profession were unhappy. Once the euphoria of profession had worn off, my doubts returned. I felt trapped and miserable. In spite of the daily kindnesses and courtesies of community life I was very solitary in spirit and felt unable to ask anyone for help. Something was wrong, and though I couldn't see it clearly, there was a radical untruth in the way I was trying to live. The trouble was that a false opposition existed for me between holiness and a thoroughgoing use of the mind. Just before entering the monastery I had been awarded a State Scholarship for Oxford; the news came after I had made my plans and fixed the date. I had to choose. Humanly speaking it might have been a lot more sensible to put off entering for a few years and use the scholarship first, but I didn't see it that way then. I thought it was a seduction and that I would lose my vocation if I didn't follow it at once. So I somehow got on to the wrong foot about the whole business of study and intellectual life: just because I felt so strongly drawn to it I thought that for me it was a siren voice; that if I was really going to go the whole hog in loving God I must resolutely 'give all that up'. This policy had worked for a while, in the novitiate – probably indeed it was a necessary stage – but after profession I became more and more intellectually frustrated, stagnant, unhappy. It would probably have become intolerable, but the Abbess rescued me and set me to thorough theological study. I had not sought it in any way; it had come through obedience. So it must be right, incredibly. I plunged in.

The change was terrific. I felt myself again and had room to grow and live. There was a great sense of inner freedom and things fell into place. I discovered the inbuilt asceticism of study: how you have to be prepared to stick at it very singlemindedly, using every little bit of time you can legitimately scrape; how you have to bring your best to it each time, even when you don't feel in the mood or are not interested in this particular section; how you have to struggle with your mental laziness; how you have to be endlessly humble before the truth, accepting your disappointments and failures but turning them to good account by learning from them, and letting go of your cherished illusions and pet theories when it becomes obvious that the evidence will not support them. But all these painful experiences were the *right* asceticism; my assumption of incompatibility between simplicity and intelligence, between dedication to contemplative prayer and a formed mind, between spiritual life and intellectual life, had trapped me in the wrong asceticism, the kind that is not death for the sake of life, but a mere narrowing and shrivelling of the spirit.

Scripture came alive. I found that I had a flair for it and felt spiritually at home in the world of the Bible. There was no conflict or even tension between hard study of the history, language and archaeological background on the one hand and the directly spiritual and theological riches on the other. There was a sense of unity and integration, and Scripture became a main source of life for me. It has remained so ever since. I identified readily and instinctively with certain characters: with Moses wanting to see God's glory, Jacob wrestling with God in the dark, Mary Magdalene at the tomb, blind Bartimaeus in the tenth chapter of Mark trying to come to Jesus (and, interestingly, being at first impeded by the crowd, then supported by it, in his endeavour!), the disciples walking to Emmaus with the risen Christ who, known yet unknown, opened the Scriptures and revealed the Easter mystery to them.

I began to be aware that we are called to love the Lord God with all our heart and with all our soul and with all our mind. I knew that truth was calling to me at every level and that to honour it was akin to worship and love. It called in every experience from the most sublime to the most mundane and domestic. It demanded intellectual integrity, the willingness to go on growing and keep my mind open to new facts or ideas even when they were disturbing, and the refusal to settle down in one corner of reality and make that the whole. Equally it demanded sincerity and humanity in relationships, self-acceptance, and obedience to the pull of God in prayer as I tried to stand before him in the truth of my poverty. This awareness of the call of truth has never left me, however I have faltered and fallen short in my response to it. Always it is bound up with love, with being set free to love and be loved, and so with vulnerability and community (on which more later).

It is bound up too with an intuition I have about judgement. 'The word of God is alive and active. It cuts more keenly than any two-edged sword, piercing as far as the place where life and spirit, joints and marrow, divide. It sifts the purposes and thoughts of the heart. There is nothing in creation that can hide from him; everything lies naked and exposed to the eyes of the One with whom we have to reckon' (Heb. 4.12–13, NEB). What is this picture – an animal with neck stretched out for sacrifice, or a surgeon's table, or what? Anyway, it is at first sight chilling and looks like a concrete representation of the general human fear of standing under God's judgement: Adam absconds into the shrubbery rather than face it; people tremble at the thought of the last assize when 'everything will come out'. But that is only half the truth, or much less than half. A more important reality comes across in Psalm 138 (139), where to stand under God's creative, judging, loving gaze is the creature's ultimate peace:

> O Lord, you search me and you know me . . .
> Where can I go from your spirit,
> or where can I flee from your face? . . .
> It was you who created my being,
> knit me together in my mother's womb.
> I thank you for the wonder of my being . . .

That marvellous psalm has meant a great deal to me all through my monastic life. The creature longs to be transparent to God, finds ecstasy and joy and peace in being wholly loved. Death and judgement in their innermost secret are not going to be terror, I believe, but pure joy and relief. Painful, yes, but what we most deeply want. It is like Peter facing Jesus on the lakeside after the resurrection, looking into the same eyes which had turned towards him in the high priest's courtyard after his denial; and saying, 'Lord, you know everything; you know that I love you.' But it is not only at the end that we stand under God's gaze like this: we do so now whenever we consent in prayer to be there in the truth of our poverty and sinfulness before him, whenever we try to face the truth and honour it in relationships with other people and in life generally. Truth has a cleansing power and we are made for it. We are having our purgatory now in the measure that we are willing to abide in it before God, judged and cleansed, loved and re-created.

To get back to the story. In these years – my early thirties –in spite of the growth just mentioned (or perhaps because of it) things got harder in other ways. Celibacy became much tougher, because I now had a much fuller appreciation of what I had 'given up', especially at the level of companionship. I was very lonely. This was not the community's fault, either then or later; it was probably due to my extreme shyness, but it was real. I battled a lot with the mystery of virginity: how an apparently love-curtailing, life-denying call could really be a means to greater love. Such glimmerings as were gained came in useful later when some of us had to write a book called *Consider Your Call*, on the monastic vocation in general, but there could not be 'answers'. Christian virginity is not a problem to be solved but a mystery to be lived and is inseparable from the Easter mystery as a whole.

At this time came the Second Vatican Council and I was repeatedly impressed by the discovery that the outside and the inside, the life of the Church and my own life, were astonishingly in tune. Each day in the refectory we used to read the reports of the speeches and acts of the conciliar fathers on the preceding day, and I had a series of shocks at hearing that high-ranking prelates had said in the debates what I had been thinking in my secret heart about the Church for years, but had supposed that I shouldn't be thinking. This sounds arrogant, perhaps, but it was true. The Church of the Second Vatican Council was being called by the Spirit away from legalism into a new trust in God, into a sense of mystery and an awareness that his mercy is greater than our categories. The Church was being called away from the kind of loyalty to its Founder which seemd to imply that it had all the answers and could not admit to not having them without letting the side down, towards an openness to receive from other Christians and a freedom to admit that they might sometimes have the mind of Christ, and this without compromising the essentials of its faith. From the remains of a power-structure and the habit of defending its privilege it was called to be the Servant Church, the Church of poverty, the Church of sinners; vulnerable, open and governed by the ever-surprising word of God. A theological approach and mentality often fairly remote from Scripture was giving way to a theology that lived very consciously on the scriptural message of salvation history; this shift was very evident in some Council documents, particularly those on the Church and on Divine Revelation. The Church was now not so much a fortress to be defended, an ark of salvation, a perfect society; it was more inclined to see itself as a sacramental sign of salvation for all, and as a pilgrim. To give these examples may seem to polarize positions too much, for things are never so clear-cut in real life, but there was a powerful movement of the Spirit in all this which touched chords in me. I knew that what I was feeling towards, groping and hoping for in my own life, was what the Church itself was feeling towards, groping and hoping for. I knew that the same Spirit was stirring the longings at these different levels and I had an enormous sense of identification with the searching Church, the Church of joy and hope and tension, the Church called by the Spirit to trust and openness.

This experience suggests something to me about the place of monastic life in the whole life of God's people. I cannot understand my vocation in purely individual terms, highly personal though it is. I have already mentioned that the Easter perspective is primordial for me: in many ways and at many levels I experience my life as a sharing with Christ in his suffering, death, resurrection and communication of the Spirit; if this were not the case, monastic life would make no sense to me. Yet to say this is to make no claim to any special monastic prerogative, for it is in every Christian that Christ lives out his mysteries, in every Christian that the Church is present and alive. At most one could say that certain features of monastic observance – particularly listening to the word of Scripture, the daily celebration of the liturgy and the experience of close-knit community – foster such an awareness and make it explicit. It seems to me that the meaning of the monastic vocation is to be sought not on the periphery but in the centre of Christian life, indeed of human life and experience.

At about the time the Second Vatican Council ended, I was appointed novice mistress and held the job for nine years. It was a complex experience. In some ways it was joy: there was all the dynamism of the Council; I had a feeling of being fully used, of being in a job where I could give all I had to give; there was the work with people and some lasting friendships were established. But there was also, especially in the later years, a sharp sense of personal inadequacy for the work. I helped a few people, but others not at all, and I ended up with a general sense of failure. I am heartily glad that I was taken off the job, although at the time it was a wrench, a little death.

During these years the charismatic renewal became very influential in the community. It highlighted much that needed to be re-emphasized and rediscovered, and brought a more explicit sense of community and mutual support. For me, however, this sense was as yet very imperfect and tended to be confined to the like-minded, those on the same wavelength. I was still pretty solitary inside, shy and afraid. I made the astonishing discovery that my shyness and fear were sometimes mistaken for self-sufficiency. Nevertheless the renewal led us to expect the healing power of the Lord in persons and situations and to understand healing as a community task. I came to see that nearly everybody carries inner wounds from his or her past experience; I knew that

I did myself, from things that had happened in childhood. The past episodes may have been one's own fault; they may have been innocently suffered; perhaps most often they are a confusion in which we can't sort out the one from the other. These wounded memories can cripple us in our response to love, both divine and human. But Jesus Christ is the Lord of history, and that holds also for our personal history. He can and does heal our memories, especially through the mediation and support of those who pray with us. The healing is not necessarily instant or spectacular, but it happens.

At this same time I had another experience of great significance. This was the work of the English Benedictine Congregation's Theological Commission, on which I served for years in the production of *Consider Your Call* and in other enterprises which more or less grew from that. This whole experience has been one of the most enriching of my monastic life. There were different levels to it. One was a deepening sense of the EBC tradition; it had always been important to me, but now I discovered its depth, soundness, goodness, sanity and spirituality as never before. In consequence I was much strengthened in my vocation. Then there was intellectual growth through the theological stimulation of it all, the sharing of ideas and the mutual education that went on through those years. I enjoyed the exchanges with other minds and discovered that I had some gift for theology and for writing. I came to realize how individualistic my concept of monastic life had been, how much of the EBC's theology of community had been missing. Along with this there was human growth through friendship. I experienced being accepted by the Commission, being used and loved and valued, with my strengths and weaknesses. I thoroughly enjoyed the company of men and the stimulation of it; they called out the real me and I felt able to be myself and speak my mind with them. We understood each other and the discussion of serious issues was interspersed with laughter. I remember, for instance, how late one evening when we were all tired but trying to finish some part of the work, I was reading out a piece I had written which included a quotation from St Augustine. Foolishly I said, 'That bit's Augustine, not me', and received the swift reply, amid gales of laughter from the others, 'We know you're marvellous, Maria, but we can tell the difference.'

The result of all this experience has been that in those years and subsequently the greatest friendships of my life have flowered. I have found a capacity for friendship with many people both inside and outside my own community, gained confidence in my ability to love and dared a little more to let myself be loved and known. Along with friendship has come a clear call to fullness of life. There is a sense of things broadening and an awareness that closing in on oneself is the essence of sin. Without directly seeking it, I have been given an enhanced capacity to appreciate and enjoy. A few practical descriptions of monastic life as I now experience it may help to make clear what I mean about being called to fullness of life.

Part of it is a new awareness of creation, a growing delight in living things and natural beauty. The changing seasons mean a great deal to me now and are inextricably entwined with the rhythms of the liturgy which forms the strong central movement in monastic prayer. Picking beans and tunes from the Office, smells or tastes and the great festivals, tactile sensations and the seasonal celebration of Christ's redemptive mysteries – all these are linked together in a strong web of associations. The first smell of winter in the air thrills me. I love the increasing darkness during December, when the daylight shrinks to a few half-hearted hours and the long nights are full of stars; amid all this we are singing in choir about mankind's darkness into which the Light of the World is born, about the longing of Advent and the preliminary fulfilment at Christmas when God, in whom there is no darkness, sends the Word who enlightens every man, and about the quest of Gentile kings who put their hopes in the leading of a star. While the sleep of winter still lies over everything, the snowdrops are already up and soon after them the straight spears of daffodil shoots, some of them piercing a hole right through a dead leaf from last year.

Then there is Lent, a unique medley of austerity, wonderful Scripture readings, crocuses, primroses and daffodils, bird-song and nesting, and the paschal mystery of life out of death. The rhubarb comes on surprisingly fast once the year has turned. A special atmosphere fills the monastery during Lent and one element in it is a mania for spring cleaning. I suspect that this is something very ancient and deep in the female psyche, probably a survival from the day when the first cavewoman saw the first spring sunshine slanting into the cave and turned the children outside while she cleaned the place up. At any rate, the community becomes badly obsessed with it during Lent. And as we pray silently in the early morning before Matins, the birds' dawn chorus is intensifying and filling out. Lent is God's gift to his people, a challenging gift and a needed cleansing, a call to be created anew. At Easter a wholeness and a power of life touch us, promising what we celebrate, believe in and dimly realize amid our dying existence. In the darkness of Easter night there is the strange evocation of ancient pagan rites of spring and the passing of the light to one another, the light derived from the Easter candle that stands for the risen Christ.

After Easter the atmosphere changes. The joy and triumphant peace of paschal time blend with the smell of the first grass-cutting of summer. The year moves on towards fruitfulness; and ocassionally there is the piercing delight of baby hedgehogs, unperturbed by nuns on hands and knees gazing at them or even picking them up to see what their tiny hands are like. The pheasants which inhabit our grounds produce a family. The grain fields all round slowly turn yellow. The Feast of Our Lady's Assumption in August says something about wholeness, fruit-fulness, maturity and God's final harvest.

Then comes the assault on the apple trees, an intensive programme of picking, carefully planned but constantly disrupt-ed by unfavourable weather because it is bad for the apples (not the nuns, apparently) if we pick them in the wet. The autumnal gales tend to come at this time and it is a very special sensation to feel the tree rocking under you. At one time the work used to be enlivened by young calves inspecting the boxes of picked apples at the foot of the trees; now it is cocks and hens that have to be fended off. The new apples taste so strong that they hurt your teeth for the first few days. In the middle of the apple-picking there are likely to be one or more days of potato-lifting, when every able-bodied member of the community is needed. This is hard work and intensely enjoyable. By the end of the day it feels strange to walk on level floors indoors after feeling the ridges of earth under your boots for so long; you ache all over but there is a deep satisfaction. All around us the beeches are turning gold, red and brown, and showering down their leaves to enrich the good soil yet again.

These cyclic renewals, spiritual and material, have spoken powerfully to me all through my monastic life. There is a harmony between prayer and life, a correspondence between God's creative activity within us and all round us, a sense of being caught up in a great dance. On the shorter time-scale of days and weeks it is real too, evoked by the smell of new bread, the special atmosphere of Sunday, the joy of clean clothes. Somebody once pointed out the special resonances of the word 'new' in Christianity: Christ brings us a new covenant, a new birth, a new commandment of love and the new wine of Eucharist; we are formed into one new man in him and promised a new Jerusalem, a new heaven and a new earth.

There is joy too in people, the steady certainty of stable relationships and loyalty in monastic life, and the largely unspoken love of those with whom you have shared daily life for so long. So much is understood and taken for granted that things do not always need elaborate statement. This can have its funny side. There is a notice board on which is displayed any announcement about work or domestic arrangements: anything from someone's need for scholarly reference to the vagaries of the plumbing. The notice may be very laconic, as everyone knows the background. For instance, we always have problems about heating the house in winter because of the cost of fuel and so there are severe restrictions on opening windows while the heating is on. At one period the system was that we could open them only when it was mild; on cold days they had to be kept shut. Since people's estimates of what was cold were diverse, one member of the community used to have the job of putting up a notice saying 'A cold day.' Visitors thought it curious that we needed to have it pointed out. Again, I remember how one summer there was some loose masonry in the church tower and the official in charge put up a notice asking the community not to walk in the cemetery underneath (a pleasant place of bees and trees and grass) until it had been attended to, because of the danger of falling stone. The repairs were long delayed; after months a terse notice appeared to announce their completion. Unfortunately in the meantime some guests from another monastery had arrived and were seen standing intrigued before a notice which simply stated, 'The cemetery is now safe.'

There is a wealth of shared experience among those who know they have been called to seek God, and to be found by him, together. But this is not confined to members of one community in the narrow sense; there is a common memory in God's people, a memory of his faithfulness and saving love through the ups and downs of their history. Central to monastic life is the regular celebration of the Office in common, and the Office is largely made up of psalms and other readings from Scripture. Day by day, week by week and year by year a monastic community prays the psalms in which Israel's experience of God was crystallized, and celebrates the redeeming mysteries of the Lord until he comes again. It is a dramatic and poetic celebration in a sense, yet it is far from being an aesthetic exercise; indeed, human frailty being what it is, the result is often not aesthetically beautiful at all. But we are expressing through these forms our own life with God, both individual and corporate, and as we pray we are identified with God's people in every century and every place. The themes and moments of Israel's history are transposed. The desert march of the Israelites prefigures Christ's combat in the wilderness and the long trek of the pilgrim Church, as well as the desert confrontation between the individual who prays and God. The exodus of Israel is a type of Christ's exodus from the prison-house of death, of every Christian's sharing in his Easter victory through baptism, and of the lifelong effort to make real in daily life what was once done for us sacramentally. It is our own story that we relive in the liturgy and it is the Church's story; the two cannot be clearly separated. To live with the robust earthiness of the psalms and the strong objective spirituality of the Scriptures as one's daily bread is an education like no other. Everything comes into focus here: nature, creation and Easter; the experience of God's people, the sense of history and personal vocation; the joy of community life and some of its sharpest agonies. Continually we are stretched, lifted above our petty concerns and challenged to pray in faith. Continually we fail, but the rhythm flows on, the river of Christ's prayer that carries us along.

This call to fuller life which I have heard has also meant for me some kind of new love for God the Creator and his creative act itself. It is difficult to put this into words without sounding naïve or anthropomorphic, but it seems to me significant. The creation stories in Genesis make a strong appeal to me and so does the fantastic and unimaginably long story of the evolution of life. I spoke earlier of my favourite Psalm 138 (139); that psalmist, I think, knew what it means to stand within God's creative power and creative love:

> Already you knew my soul,
> my body held no secret from you
> when I was being fashioned in secret
> and moulded in the depths of the earth.

(vv. 14–15)

In the depths of the earth, from the sea and the mud, through primitive life-forms for millions and millions of years, through the small, discreet mammals which proved more successful than the great dinosaurs, through the hominids and the quiet but all-important step to being human, through the two or three million years of man's adventure on earth. Conscious of himself, he can stand before God, worshipping:

> For it was you who created my being,
> knit me together in my mother's womb.

I thank you for the wonder of my being,
for the wonders of all your creation.

(ibid., vv. 13–14)

I remember the awe with which I first discovered St Thomas Aquinas's theology of creation. Creation is the issuing of the whole being of a thing from the universal cause, which is God. It is not the turning of something into this or that, the transformation of some given raw material, as all our 'creativity' is, for without him there is simply nothing. God-Who-Is is himself the Author of the creature's existence in every dimension, its being as such, not just its being this or that. And God's creative causality is not confined to the moment when we begin to be; it extends to every moment of our existence. If I were not sustained by him at this moment at the very root of my being, I would fall back into my native nothingness. As Julian of Norwich said, creation 'would fall to naught for littleness' (*Revelations*, ch. 5). To me this truth is sheer joy. His creation of you is not something that happened once, *x* many years ago; he is still at it. His healing, creative hands are upon your body, upon your mind, upon that fine point of your spirit where his likeness is stamped on you – not a static likeness but an evolving reality. The whole strength of his loving will is in that creative act by which he wants you, loves you, rejoices in your being; and you can let yourself go in joyful agreement with his creative will, saying with Jesus, 'Father, into your hands I commit my spirit.' When I was a child my father's hands meant a great deal to me. They were the most beautiful hands I have ever seen: large, beautifully shaped, strong, very sensitive and kind. I have many memories of clinging to them, but one recurrent joy stands out, that of being bathed by him as a small child. He used to run plenty of water into the bath, and make it very soapy and then put his child in. He scorned flannels, sponges and other impediments and did the whole job with his hands, caressing the child all over. At the time I simply enjoyed it with a mixture of sensuous delight and love; since then the memory of it has become for me a kind of sacrament of resting in the loving, cleansing, healing, creative hands of God.

When you are before God in prayer, you are consenting to his creation of you in the depths of your being, consenting precisely to his creation in you of the relationship we call 'prayer'. He creates in you the longing for union with him because it is first his longing. Your existence is his word of love; your desire for him is acquiescence in the love that loved first. Your 'naked intent unto

God' unleashes in you the creative Spirit of whom you are only partially aware, somewhat in the same way that the celebration of the sacraments in faith unleashes in you the dynamism of the paschal mystery, the dying and being reborn.

His incessant creative action is bringing us to a wholeness in which his project of love will be made perfect, and this means that he is the Healer. 'See, I lift never mine hands off my work, nor ever shall, without end,' said the Lord to Julian of Norwich (ibid., ch. 11); and in the fifth chapter of John's Gospel Jesus speaks of God's unending creative activity: 'My Father is working still, and I am working.' This statement is part of the discourse attached to an act of healing. I think we are dimly aware at times of the challenge to be open to his continuous work of healing, his call to wholeness.

To illustrate this, here are a couple of images which have meant a lot to me. I am not the type who is favoured with interesting and meaningful dreams. I used to think that I never dreamed at night at all, except that they say everyone does, but one forgets them. However, twice in my life I have had beautiful dreams, which I looked on as gifts. They were given, I think, in about 1975 and 1976, some months apart.

The first one I have already described in *Marked for Life*, but I called it a parable there, being shy of admitting that it was a dream. I was on the flat, spacious roof of a high building, with a low parapet round the edge. Some friends, not clearly identified but known as adult friends, were walking to and fro with me, and we were discussing some grave matter. Near us was a little boy of about five or six, a very beautiful child and extremely joyful and lively. He ran ahead and back again, lagged behind and then caught up; he called out to us to play with him and tried in every way to attract our attention. We were too engrossed in our grave discussion to notice or have time for him. Then he ran ahead and jumped up on to the parapet and stood there with his back to the terrible drop, laughing. My friends gasped with horror and lunged forward to seize him lest he fall. I remained still, because I had begun to understand. Before they could grab him he laughed, waved and jumped off backwards. The friends were appalled, but I somehow knew (from a brief earlier scene, I think) that on the face of the building, out of our line of vision but visible to the boy as he stood on the parapet, was some scaffolding, and on it stood the boy's father. So I knew he was all right. Then the scene shifted; I was still on the roof but the friends had gone. The boy was back and I was alone with him. He thought it was a marvellous game, this jumping off, and he did it again and again

as I watched, sometimes forward, sometimes backwards, sometimes looking first and sometimes not, but always with delight.
He was overflowing with life and joy and he wanted me to play
with him. I never saw his father, but could guess what the father
must be like from the relationship the boy clearly had with him,
his certainty of being safely caught. Eventually I decided to play
too . . . but it was time to get up.

This left me feeling enormously happy and the more I thought
about it the more depths there seemed to be. The most evident is
this: no man has ever seen God, but the only Son, who is nearest
to the Father's heart, has made him known. Christ falls into
death, but in so doing he commits himself into the Father's hands
and lives again. We could not make this leap, could not commit
our spirit into the Father's hands, unless Christ had done so first
and invited us to go with him. Very prominent was the fact that
he did it not grimly, with clenched teeth, but alight with love and
joy. Then there are further meanings. When you are with faceless
friends in a dream, so I have heard, the 'friends' are aspects of
yourself that have split off. If this is true, the dream is a story of
integration: the friends were there (separated off) at the
beginning, but absent (or integrated) at the end. At first they kept
me from attending to the boy, but after his leap I was no longer
divided and could give myself up to his game. At first there was
preoccupation with the grave concerns of self-important adults
who had no time for play; after the boy's leap I wanted to play
with him. Finally there is the ancient archetype of the myths, the
Miraculous Child who plays for ever, image of resurrection, new
life, new possibility and the child in yourself. This image occurs
again in the Wisdom literature of the Old Testament: when the
Creator was at his first work, says Wisdom:

> Then I was at his side each day,
> his darling and delight,
> playing in his presence continually,
> playing on the earth, when he had finished it,
> while my delight was in mankind.

> (Prov. 8.30–31, NEB)

Play is akin to dance, for dancing is the play of adults, and
both are signs of wholeness. Dancing was the theme of the
second dream. I was in some kind of large hall and the Lord was
there in visible form, though I had no clear idea of what he looked
like. I was very pleased that he was there and my instinct was to
dance for him. So I began, making up my dance as I went along,

thoroughly enjoying it and aware that he was enjoying it too. I danced and danced with great joy. Even in the dream I had the realization: Isn't this marvellous, that he has given me such freedom that I can dance before him and *enjoy* it! This dream made me understand that one day we shall be so whole, so trusting, so free in our love for God and one another that our inhibitions will fall away. And when that comes it will be sheer gift. Whenever a certain psalm verse turns up in the Office I think of it:

> For me you have changed my mourning into dancing,
> you removed my sackcloth and girdled me with joy.

> (Ps. 29 (30). 12 (11))

I have sometimes glimpsed, just a little, what it would mean if I really let God's creative love make me, heal me without obstruction and flow through me to others. I have come to understand Benedictine life as a call to listen to the creative word of God and I hear it especially in Scripture and in the liturgy, in nature and in prayer. But more and more it has come home to me that we hear God's word only if we are prepared to be non-selective about where we hear it; and one of the surest places where he speaks is in community life. It is not only what people say, though times without number I have been conscious of God gently making me understand something through conversation with one of the community, or a guest. Over the years, however, I have also become conscious of body-language, of how much members of the community 'speak' by the way they walk and work, react and relax, handle books and wash dishes. St Benedict says in his famous chapter on humility that by the time a monk has completed the arduous climb, by the time the emptying-out of selfishness is achieved in him, his humility will be unmistakably evident to all from his very bearing. Lately it has been borne in on me how true this is; living very close to people one becomes aware of the unselfish kindness, the predictable integrity, in all they do. This is a word of the Lord to me, even when nothing is said. Monastic life in community can be a very creative thing, if we allow it to be.

There is a ministry of the word outside the community as well, and on this I want to say something. The years of collaboration on *Consider Your Call*, the way the book was received and various speaking and writing jobs in which I have been involved in connection with that, have made me understand that communication of the word is part of my vocation, even though I am not a priest. More and more I have been invited to speak and write and share ideas; I have never angled for these invitations but have always been asked in ways that made me think it was the Lord whom I obeyed when I responded. This is not to say that I have been immune to failure, far from it; but failures too can be within his plan. A surprising event in this development came when as part of the arrangements for St Benedict's centenary in 1980 I was invited to Australia and Japan to talk to communities of men and women there who live by the same Rule. In consequence of this I went all round the world. The whole experience was a marvellous gift of shared joy, inspiration, mind-stretching and new friendships. It would take another book to describe it, but there is one incident I could pick out. On my first night in Tokyo I woke up in the small hours with a strange, tense feeling and then the bed began to rock around. It was like the bombing of London when I was a child in the Second World War, but this was an earthquake. For the first few seconds, being inexperienced in earthquakes, I thought we were all going to die (although no one in the house bothered to get up) and I remember thinking that an act of contrition would be appropriate. But no words at all would come, except 'Glory be to the Father and to the Son and to the Holy Spirit', so I offered that, hoping it would be acceptable even if not quite right. The first tremor passed and I had time to collect my wits before the second, so then I said a proper act of contrition. But uppermost in my mind was the thought that if I had only a few more minutes to live, I didn't want to waste them talking to God about my sins. He knew all that, and I mainly wanted to thank him for all the love, all the joy.

That long journey round the world points up for me the paradox, the surprising quality of God's dealings with us. One enters an enclosed monastery, through the 'narrow gate', only to find oneself years later being sent round the world, to 'the lands of sunrise and sunset'; one 'gives up' so much at the human level, and it is poured back: a fullness of life, wide horizons and the gift of undreamed friendships. I never experience this outgoing activity as in any sense conflicting or competing with the inwardness and silence. The word that is spoken is the word that has first been listened to; if not, it will be only 'sound and fury, signifying nothing'. The inwardness seems to demand the communication, and vice versa. This gives rise to reflections on the meaning of 'contemplative monastic life': I wonder, for instance, whether it is not more threatened by excessive human isolation than by excessive human contact, in the case of some enclosed nuns. But this is not the place to develop the point.

This brings me back to the matter of community. All along, there has been the challenge of community and I have never really learned how to meet it. To borrow an idea expressed by Abbot Victor Farwell, community life goes on at three levels. On the surface there is pleasant conversation, social intercourse, chit-chat. At the deepest, there is the common conviction that we are all going to God and our lives belong to him. In between these two there is the level of deep human and spiritual exchanges, the plane at which we entrust ourselves to one another by articulating our convictions and our feelings about things that matter most. Perhaps a similar description could be given of the 'community' of married life. It is easy to be at peace about the top and bottom levels. The real challenge is the middle one: this is where fear and distrust divide, where people feel threatened. This is where I am afraid that what I say, think and am will be scorned, what I hold precious will not be valued. This is where I am afraid of 'the common life', where I am tempted to shirk the issue and keep all but a very few out of my well-guarded world.

It is so much easier to operate like this, to seem to be a good community member because you live a good life and are nice to people and work hard and pray most earnestly; but you are in practice going it alone. You have in your heart of hearts given up on the community as such, even though you love individuals. I have come to see that this is, in my own life, basically dishonest. It is like leaving; one just 'leaves' in a more face-saving way than a person who goes off slamming the door. If I really opted for this as a way of life (as opposed to the temporary makeshift which is the best I can do for the moment) I should be cynically refusing both the deepest challenge and the surest revelation of God that is made to us in monastic life.

All the same, there is genuine suffering in community life, as in marriage, which is not to be simply condemned as a refusal of the challenge and the revelation. A person can be aware that the level of life and communication is not perfect and yet be unable to do anything directly about it. If that is where you are, the suffering you accept in this situation is redemptive, because it is a share in the experience of Christ. The moment in his life when he was enabling true love and communion to happen between human beings was the moment when he was utterly alone, on the cross. There is an element of loneliness, of real 'dying', in any life where people are trying to learn love and this suffering is for the brethren, for the Body. It is important not to confuse real Christian community with 'creating good relationships' on a psychological level.

All the lifelines of meaning that I have been trying to trace in this story seem to converge towards community, so if I am not prepared to try to live them out precisely here, at the heart of community life, their validity is called in question. For example, I have from my earliest days in the monastery seen prayer and the monastic vocation as a sharing in Christ's paschal mystery; but just as God is revealed in the suffering face of Christ, so also is he to be seen in the suffering face of the community, in service and the washing of one another's feet and vulnerability and forgiveness. Again, monastic life is listening to the word, exposure to the word, and on occasion speaking it; but where am I prepared to hear it? Only in Scripture, liturgy, reading, theology, nature, poetry . . . or also in the 'most patient bearing', of the brethren's infirmities and my own? Monastic life is supposed to be about the experience of God in some sense; but am I prepared for the searing, humbling, anger-provoking, frustrating experience that life in choir can sometimes be, where I experience among other things that I am not God? And then, joy in creation: yes, but can I really take it when all these odd bits of God's creation, so scandalously unlike me, are the place where his glory is revealed? And healing – yes, but I find it pretty difficult to receive healing through Christ's Body, if that means his here-and-now Body. Creativity: will he let me, in the long run, shrink away from the painful, humbling task of being used as an instrument of his new-creation project in the community, and this when I often feel despairing about real renewal in large and venerable institutions?

I take comfort from a certain powerful symbol. In my community we use at Mass hosts baked from wholemeal flour; they are not the smooth, uniform, white wafers of one's youth, but have a beautiful homespun roughness. We take it in turns to do the Offertory procession. When it is my week I study the plateful as I carry it up the choir. No single host is perfect, nor like any other. There are speckled ones, flawed ones, chipped ones, dark ones; there are rough bits and excrescences and cracks. A picture of the community. But when we arrive at the sanctuary, they are not scorned as rejects; Christ graciously accepts them, to turn them into his Body.

Some Themes

Big tapestries, they say, look terrible from the back, especially while they are still in the making. You can see only a jumble of colours, scores of loose ends and knots; no coherent pattern is discernible, only a mess. But when you go round to the front, there it all is: hunting scenes and battle scenes, enemies' heads rolling in the moat and people in gardens picking bright fruit from ornamental trees.

God does not show us much of the pattern this side of death; we can only believe that he is making something finally beautiful out of the mess and confusion that life presents from this side. Yet we do get some imperfect glimpses of parts of the pattern and I can pick out three or four from my story as I have told it.

The first is obvious. It is the interplay between being on one's own and being in a community, or between having an interior life and searching for human love and communion. The contemplative pull grows stronger: the pull of the desert, the call to abandon oneself in faith to the mystery of God, the need for prayer and surrender. But these things entail, not as a kind of compensatory balance but as an exigency of their innermost meaning, a venturing outwards in human love. If it is *Christian* contemplation with which we are concerned, then there can be no ultimate conflict (though there may be superficial tension) between the contemplative elements in monasticism and the simultaneous challenge to let love cast out fear, to be open and trusting and vulnerable with people, to be healed and to accept the pain of knowing and being known, loving and being loved.

The second is that I can only begin to understand this if I see it in the paschal perspective. The grain of wheat dies and there is a new creation. Christian life, monastic life, is a series of little deaths and anticipatory resurrections, but we should not understand this if we had not seen it first in Christ. Over the years I have become increasingly aware of identification with Christ as the discoverer of the Father, with Christ as the Way and not only the goal. The bafflement and sense of failure that we go through all the time, in prayer and in the whole of life, are our insertion into his experience. In our blundering and disillusion-ment, our failure and weakness and inconsistencies, he is living out again his own Easter passage to perfect obedience, his own long-matured act of surrender into the Father's hands. If this is true – and I am more and more convinced that it is – then the Easter glory cannot be entirely some deferred thing; it must be present now as the secret meaning of a great deal of our daily experience. The signs of the new creation are already with us and we know, intermittently and obscurely, the wholeness that is to come.

The third pattern I have seen is the gentleness of God's dealings, and in particular the revelation of his gentleness in the heart of dread, or grief or shock. It has come home to me twice in connection with the death of people I loved. The first time it was my father. I had had, all my life, a relationship with him too beautiful to describe; he was to me a sacrament of God's fatherhood that nothing could ever replace. After I had become a nun I used sometimes to think with dread of how one day he would be dying and all my brothers and sisters would be there but I would be unable to go (this was before the Second Vatican Council, and the enclosure rules were very rigid). The thought was horrible and I used to turn it over to the Lord very deliberately, as something I couldn't handle, but he could. Then one day it happened: the sudden phone call to say that my father was dying, the sick feeling of helplessness. It was agony. A little later I rang up to find out how he was and to my astonishment was put straight through to my father himself; he had had an extension put in and the phone was beside his bed – I hadn't known. So he said goodbye to me on his deathbed, unselfish and cheerful as ever, and died a few hours later. I was overwhelmed by the tenderness of it; it had never entered my head to pray for that.

There is a prayer in the liturgy that has always moved me. It occurs now on the 27th Sunday of the Year:

> Almighty, everliving God, in your overflowing
> love for us who pray to you, you go further than
> we deserve, further even than we know how to
> desire. Pour out on us your mercy, forgiving
> those things our conscience dreads and heaping
> upon us what our prayer does not venture to ask.

That prayer has always seemed to me remarkably close to the heart of things, and the experience just mentioned brought it home anew.

The second time that God's gentleness came home to me in this special way was at the death of my priest brother. He was in hospital with heart trouble but was supposed to be recovering. I went to see him. It was all joy, good talk and laughter. His doctor said that, in view of his improvement, he could say Mass next morning, for the first time since his illness began. He himself pulled all strings and made all arrangements to get me present at his Mass in the hospital chapel before I caught my train back to Stanbrook. It was a votive Mass of our Lady, and I read the first lesson; it included the passage about Wisdom playing in creation, which I have quoted in connection with my parapet dream. After Mass we said goodbye and, full of thankfulness, I left him. He died suddenly about three hours later. The shock was very great, yet the mercy and tenderness at the heart of it all overwhelmed me. It is as though God sometimes has to use a great shock to break our hearts open to his gentleness. Then the cross and the glory are not two separate moments; we know the glory in the midst of the pain.

This encounter with gentleness has been, especially on the two occasions just described but also more generally along my path, one of the surest experiences of God. His gentle touch stills us, shocks us, as with Elijah in the cave. The revelation of a tenderness so much greater than we deserve takes the wind out of our sails and shatters our trite ideas of God as nothing else can; and I think it is one of the most genuinely and joyfully humbling experiences I have ever known.

This brings me to the last of the pattern-threads I can see, and that is the nearness of eternal life. In the moments when God touches us so gently, we know eternity not as some remote, unimaginable existence but as the consummation of all that is most true and real in our human experience. The best insights we have ever known, in ourselves and in one another, are going to prove the truest in the end. I have known very much joy, have been given very much of love and life. In my most human intuitions I am aware that the joys I do not grab or cling to, the beauty I salute and honour, the love I receive and give again, are indestructible. We let go of them now, when they are taken from us by separations or death, but they remain pure, eternal and laid up in promise. We know then something of the tension of which the saints have spoken, the tension between longing for that eternal life for which we are manifestly made and awareness of how much remains to be done here. Friendship has revealed this nearness of eternity to me more clearly than any other experience, so that the Communion of Saints is not so much a doctrine held as an experience already shared. What we have known in love and friendship is too great to be self-explanatory in terms of this life alone.

This means that the intuitions I had about the place of monastic life in the Church which is Christ's Body, and about the paschal mystery as penetrating monastic life – intuitions most vital to me at the beginning of my vocation – are present still, but they are with me now in a more humanly experienced way. They have taken flesh for me; they are to some imperfect degree lived from the inside. I hope this does not sound as though I thought I knew all the answers; that is far from the truth. I am more conscious than ever of weakness, bafflement, disillusion, failure, sinfulness and real doubts. At one level there is no sureness, no security, no guarantees, but only a blundering on. We are totally unsure of ourselves and God is increasingly mysterious. Yet just as we know our purgatory now, as we stand under the gaze of his love in our sinfulness, so also, in some dim but real sense, we know our heaven.

Thank you, Father, for your faithful love that has called me and borne with me all through this journey. I'm constantly astonished that you don't give up on me, and yet I know you won't. It isn't just that you put up with me, Lord, as I disappoint you time after time; it's much more positive than that. You make me understand that in some way the failures are part of your plan. You can contain failures. You use them for our growth, like good manure. You are not going to be baulked in your love.

When I think I am standing before you, trying to pray, I often know that the reality is something other. It's not a matter of me trying to serve you, to love others, for your sake, to work for them and for you and to pray to you. No, somehow that's not right, because you are much closer than that. At the spring of my longing, you are longing; in the stretch of my understanding, you are there in your truth. In my joy, you dance in your threefold delight. The rest is silence.

Love Bade me Welcome

DOM ALAN REES

It would be difficult to describe my feelings on 4 September 1968 as we drove up the Abergavenny Road to Belmont. In one way, the story had begun in Hereford Cathedral many years before when I had bought a little book of prayers for young people written by a Mirfield Father. From this I had learned to make the sign of the cross and to build a 'holy corner' in my room in which to pray. Now, at the age of twenty-seven, I was returning to Hereford to begin my novitiate at Belmont Abbey.

I was brought up in a nominally Christian family. My father's family were strongly nonconformist, but he himself went to chapel only for 'big meetings'. My mother's family never seemed to go to any church on a regular basis; it was with them that I spent my early years, which coincided with the Second World War. My grandfather was a steelworker but he was often at home because he was asthmatic. He was a self-educated man and I spent many childhood hours sitting next to him as he taught me to draw, paint, write in copperplate style and do arithmetic. While I received this homespun tuition a spiral of smoke would rise out of the pyramid of Potter's Asthma Powder, as a relief for his tight chest and to the annoyance of the rest of us.

Since my parents had no real commitment to churchgoing, all my attraction towards religion came from occasional visits to churches and cathedrals; I seemed to be drawn to God by these visits and to be filled with gentle impressions of his presence in these old buildings. I was sent to a Welsh Baptist Sunday School where we learned to read (but not understand) the Bible in Welsh. I had no sense of God's presence in the chapel and even now I get the same feeling of absence whenever I enter such a building.

My mother occasionally took me to the local Anglican church: she knew no Welsh, so nonconformist worship was unattractive to her. When I was ten, we began to attend church regularly and I found Anglicanism most appealing, so my mother and I were confirmed together and became regular communicants. I loved the ordered worship, the singing, the devotional atmosphere of the early Communion Service, and I knew at the age of twelve that I had to give myself to God as a clergyman. I was very receptive and, at the age of fourteen, I found myself playing an active part in church life as deputy organist, chorister, server and Sunday School teacher. The Vicar lost no time in involving me, thus giving me a remote preparation for the life I wanted to embrace. I used to pray in my little prayer corner, which altered its place and aspect the more Catholic doctrine I learned. My prayers were mainly from books and from the Anglican liturgy of Matins and Evensong, and without noticing it I breathed in the Scriptures from these Prayer Book services. In a way, all this has been a firm foundation for the monastic life to which God called me later on, although I often wonder whether temperamentally I would have been better suited to a vicarage!

Catholic teaching became more prominent when I first met a Religious, an Anglican Franciscan, Fr Silyn Roberts, SSF, at a youth week at Lampeter. This was a devastating experience both of a loving Christian community of young people and of the basic elements of Catholicism. Here I made my first confession (rather poorly, in retrospect), was totally captivated by the office of Compline and bought a rosary in the local Catholic church, which we entered with some caution. During the week I learned for the first time the glory of friendship and how it transcends all barriers of age, sex and religion. God was teaching me and I was responding. I was very happy. The church became central in my life; Lampeter had made me Anglo-Catholic and I had a new world to explore. I loved the ceremonies of the liturgy and the music, but the sacramental life of frequent communion and confession coupled with the prayer of the hours and personal prayer, now enriched by devotion to our Lady and visits to her shrine at Walsingham, were central for me. I became organist in a neighbouring Anglo-Catholic church and the teaching and example of the parish priest helped me to accept all things Catholic with ease. Rome, once foreign and remote, became suddenly nearer. Rome was beckoning and I felt myself taking a hesitant step in that direction.

Anglo-Catholicism wasn't to last. A friend of mine was on the way into the Catholic Church and he introduced me to a Catholic priest, an Irishman, Fr Tom Nulty, who was full of zeal and good humour and given to plain speaking. He told me that I was barking up the wrong tree and that I needed the truth and the fullness of the Catholic faith. If I were an evangelical Christian, I would say that I 'came under the conviction of the Holy Spirit' as a result of that meeting. I remember vividly the certainty, yet the horror, of the whole situation. That was the first time I prostrated myself in prayer. I knew that I had to do God's will however difficult it might be, particularly for my parents, who were somewhat suspicious of Catholics.

At this time I met a Nashdom monk and was totally captivated by the Benedictine idea. I don't think I quite understood what it meant; I just felt it was the life for me. It was an inner call which would take years to work out.

What made me certain of God's leading at that stage was that when I broached the subject of my becoming a Catholic to my mother, she told me that in the middle of a difficult birth she had promised me to God if we should both come through safely. She felt that she could never have any objections where my religious leanings were concerned; her only intention was to honour the promise she had made to God. I felt humbled when she told me this and knew in my heart that I must never put up any obstacles to God's will for me – wherever it might lead.

My father didn't respond so positively to my desire to become a Catholic (I was just sixteen); in fact he was rather distressed, as he had recently been attending church and was being prepared for confirmation. It took him several years to accept the idea but in the end, especially after my mother's death, he always came to Mass with me and loved to visit Belmont. He remained faithful to his newly-found Anglicanism – he knew only the Catholic variety – and right up to his death he always spent time, morning and evening, in prayer. Here I saw the gentleness of God in dealing with my father and firmly keeping hold of him when he could have been alienated by my youthful determination to become a Catholic.

I was received into the Church in my first term at University College, Cardiff, making my profession of faith and confession to Dom Leo Caesar, monk of Ampleforth, who was then chaplain to the Catholic students. I had lodgings in the Benedictine parish of St Mary's where I attended daily Mass, sang in the choir and helped with the organ-playing. The Benedictine link was strengthened at home in Swansea where I attended St David's, then served by the community of Douai Abbey. In both places I was received with the utmost kindness.

I loved the early morning Masses and the time I was able to spend in prayer before getting back to digs for breakfast. I don't remember much about the content of my prayer except that the St Andrew Daily Missal figured prominently. I made some abortive attempts at meditation but was not very good at constructing scenes. I didn't ask anyone to teach me about prayer and was rather reticent about baring my soul to anyone. I felt that if I did so they would never think me a suitable candidate for the priesthood with all my sins and weaknesses (which, in retrospect, were not nearly as bad as I made out). It took many years for the Lord to break through and enable me to share myself more fully with others. I wanted to be a priest—that was certain; but I was also aware of the high demands of the priestly life, such as loneliness and celibacy. There were also so many different kinds of priests: monks, canons, Jesuits, friars, seculars, Salesians . . . *ad infinitum.* I was confused. It was so easy in the Anglican Church: one went to a theological college after graduating and then was ordained to the parochial ministry.

The confusion did not get on top of me at that time and I had plenty to keep me occupied, academically and in other ways, I had planned originally to read theology at university, but as I had now changed allegiance I thought it better to read music and this choice seems to have been richly blessed since I have been a monk. There was abundant social life in college, but I was always happiest in a small group of friends with whom I felt at ease. We were a rather closed group in the Music Faculty but there was plenty of friendship and genuine love and regard for each other. Several contemporaries either joined me in the Catholic Church (the last crop of converts before the Second Vatican Council) or became clergymen.

In my second year at university I went the rounds of the monasteries—Prinknash, Buckfast, Quarr, Ampleforth—looking for the right place in which to begin my novitiate after graduating. I made many new friends in those communities. With one of these, a dear monk, Dom Jean-Hébert Desrocquettes of Quarr, since gone to heaven, I struck up a marvellous friendship and learned that friendship is not limited by age—J.-H. D. was in his mid-seventies. At that time he was a great advocate of the Cistercian vocation: his travels in the United States, teaching chant to various Cistercian communities, had given him a great love for their way of life. All this added to my confusion. I wanted to give of my best, so was the Cistercian vocation the one for me? I panicked slightly and decided to opt for Ampleforth: here, I felt, I could get the best mixture of active and contemplative life. Abbot Byrne was very kind to me—a convert with no Ampleforth connections apart from being a term-time resident in an

Ampleforth parish – and his council accepted me for the novitiate beginning in September 1962.

For a while I was content, but it was during my finals year that I suffered my first 'desert' experience. Everything had been wonderful till then. I returned to Cardiff for the Michaelmas Term 1961 and began to suffer from insomnia. I couldn't diagnose the problem: that was left to Fr John Grimbaldestone at St David's, Swansea. He had been novice master at Douai and he quickly saw that I was still in a state of confusion. He advised me to continue with my studies and temporarily put aside all thoughts of entering the religious life until I was more settled. A letter to Abbot Byrne asking to be released from my intention brought a kind and wise reply. I then began to realize that I would no more fit into the Ampleforth novitiate than into a Cistercian novitiate – maybe the latter would have been easier.

I began to get better and regained some equilibrium before the June exams, which didn't suffer because of this upset. I am sure that there were other problems that I should have discussed with a wise director, but pride got in the way, or fear – I don't know what. I did realize that God was now in the lead, but somehow the honeymoon was over and the darkness and bafflement were very real and very painful. When I was going through my father's papers after his death, I found among them a letter I had written to my parents at that time. I had forgotten it, but it is revealing, even if a little pious:

> You have never stood in my way in my search for God. The search is still going on, but the way is very hard. I have no doubt that I will soon find him and never lose him again. My only thought in this life is to be a saint; but the road is very steep and the path narrow and dangerous. At the moment, I seem to go through one of the most darkened valleys, and although the strain is very great, I know that he is very near and that he is continually upholding me and giving me the courage to go on. I am perplexed and confused, but as Cardinal Newman says, our perplexity and confusion can serve him as well as our work and prayer, because he has made them all.
>
> I pray daily to go on in strength and courage and I feel that during the past term God has been testing my faith and is more especially doing so at the moment. I was reading St Thérèse's account of her life: 'He whose heart is watchful taught me that he works miracles even for those whose faith is like a tiny mustard seed, to make it grow, while, as in the case of his mother, he works miracles for his dearest friends only after he has tested their faith.

> He let Lazarus die, even though Martha and Mary had sent word
> that he was sick; and when he was asked by our Lady at the
> marriage feast of Cana to help the master of the house, he said his
> time had not yet come. But after the trial, what rewards! Lazarus
> rises from the dead and water becomes wine.'

What my parents could have made of this, I don't know.
They were very concerned and puzzled. The letter was written at
the lowest point of that particular period. Nevertheless, I quite
often managed to get to the early Mass, feeling totally drained
after so little sleep. I am convinced now that this was a definite
period of growth. It taught me that God is most certainly in
charge and that I shouldn't rush around organizing my own
vocation. He was doing the calling; the initiative was his. He
meant me to wait in patience until he wanted me, then I would be
ready. In the meantime there was yet more fashioning to be done:
edges to be smoothed, corners to be rounded and more
emptiness to be experienced. This first 'desert experience' taught
me obedience and patience, to wait on the Lord.

In the years between considering Ampleforth and entering
Belmont, there was a lot of wandering. After graduating, I
enrolled for the teachers' training course and then worked for five
years as a teacher in Cardiff, ending up as director of music at
Heathfield House High School for Girls where the then headmistress, Sr Mary Anthony, gave me much help and encouragement
on my path to the monastic life and the priesthood. At this time,
too, I was appointed choirmaster of St David's Cathedral,
Cardiff, where I was able to put my musical talents to the service
of the liturgy. It was here, in the early days of vernacular liturgy,
that I composed my first English setting of the Mass, 'The Mass of
St David', which was very quickly published.

In 1965 my mother died and this left a great emptiness in me.
She had been a strong support and wanted to see me a priest; her
untimely death at the age of forty-seven was a severe blow. I still
felt that I was going through a wilderness, despite the valuable
work I was doing. I felt the Lord wanted me totally for himself –
and I could be satisfied with no less. No relationship, no work, no
music could fill the emptiness. At the same time I felt I was not
giving God what he wanted: I was resisting. My daily Mass had
gone, my prayer was shallow and infrequent. I felt too unworthy
to go to Communion. I was still very interested and involved in all
that was happening in the Church, especially during the Second
Vatican Council. But within me all was not right: there were
difficulties that needed to be faced, but these were not dealt

with until later on when God opened me up more completely.

In many ways these years seemed shallow. I tended to be superficial and to skate over things too easily. I didn't have to make much effort to be reasonably successful in most areas of my life. Looking back on my university and post-university years, I recall a marvellous collection of letters from Dom Desrocquettes which I treasure. Here is an extract from one of them:

> Don't take life as: don't do that, be careful of this, I shall never do that, I cannot stand this, I feel so depressed, etc . . . but think of love, of beauty, of giving yourself, of living fully every moment of your life. Of course, don't rely on yourself for doing that. He will do it in you; your role is only to give yourself to him, to remain with him, to come back to him, like a baby, if ever by inattention or weakness you have left him for a while! Surely he loves you, this is enough to keep you happy. And if sometimes you feel miserable, think that he is still with you, looking at you, to see how you will answer him: it is just to obtain a smile from you and more love. In that way painful moments, with a little practice and the grace of God, of course, become precious for our love and our praise.

I am not sure how deeply these words penetrated my heart at that time: it is only with the passing of the years that their full effect is being realized.

My first real contact with Belmont came when I brought the boys of the cathedral choir for a working week in the summer of 1966. We lived in the school and sang our services in the Abbey Church, and I was struck by the friendliness of the brethren. Deep down I began to realize that this might be the place where I could live the monastic life, but I was not quite ready to allow these feelings to surface because just at that moment life was most enjoyable.

It was about six months later that a girl-friend of mine came to visit me. This visit is clearly imprinted in my mind. The moment of illumination came during a meal together in a very pleasant Italian restaurant in Cardiff which we nicknamed 'Pink Table-cloths'. My friend was not sure whether she was in love with someone living in the USA, so she decided to give up her work as a teacher in London and go to work near her boy-friend in the USA just to see if she was really in love with him and would marry him. She said to me, 'You are in the same position with regard to your vocation. You really do need to burn your boats and go and give it a try. Is there anywhere you find attractive?'

And then I knew that I had to let the Belmont attraction surface and give it consideration. This time I wasn't running around looking; in fact I was somewhat reluctant.

I thought and prayed until, in summer 1967, we took the boys to Belmont for another singing week. This time I had an interview with Abbot Robert Richardson and told him I would like to test my vocation at Belmont. His council accepted me for September 1968. In 1966 my father had remarried. Kit was a wonderful person who was devoted to him as he was to her. She was a nurse and well able to care for him as his health had never been good after the war. I was free to see if God wanted me to be a Benedictine monk at Belmont Abbey.

My career as cathedral choirmaster ended with a trip to Loreto with the choir to sing in an international festival of church music. Little did I imagine then that I would return there five years later as a monk, studying at Sant' Anselmo, to conduct them in a piece of Gregorian chant on their second visit. After a summer holiday in the Italian lakes, I went home briefly to say goodbye and set out for Belmont. At last I was doing something that I had longed to do for ten years, yet there was deep regret at the good things that I thought I was leaving behind. I fully believed that family, friends, music, 'life' itself would have no part in the monastic way I was choosing. What I was to find in the novitiate, and since in the monastic life, was not the outward or bodily austerities that I had feared, but something more demanding: the stripping of self, the grappling with the 'old man', the resistance within and the struggle as the Lord shaped the old into the new. The long process of discovery and of being discovered by God was truly beginning, in a fumbling but real way.

After the first weeks of novelty tinged with euphoria, the bleakness of the novitiate took hold and I began to realize just how attached I was to all sorts of things that I had just been taking for granted outside. It comes as a shock to a person used to responsibility to be rebuked for trifles by the novice master: one has to learn humility and struggle to accept a rebuke and put it into a 'spiritual context'. Another thing that quickly came home to me was the lack of freedom and the sense of being continually 'under observation'. Then there was the whole business of prayer: to come from a very basic notion of praying – or no praying at all – to a daily half-hour without any specific instruction as to what to do with it was difficult. Probably the hardest feature of the novitiate was learning to live with one's fellow novices, who were of widely differing temperaments, backgrounds and ages.

The novitiate is intended to leave one certain space for reflection and the silence and loneliness certainly made one look inward, backward, forward, occasionally upward and often downward! In the busyness of one's life in the world it was easy to skate over problems and worries or tuck them away in an unused and shadowy corner. In my case, one of these problems was the fear of death and this soon crept out. Fortunately I discovered Dom John Chapman's *Spiritual Letters* and these were a great source of comfort to me. His wisdom on the subjects of death and prayer was a sure guide. I find all sorts of jottings from the *Spiritual Letters* in my notebook. The following are typical:

> If God sees best for me to die, what in the world should one wish to live for?

> You are the block, God is the sculptor; you cannot know what He is hitting you for, and you *never will* in this life. All you want is patience, trust, confidence and He does it all. It is very simple – simplicity itself . . . Let it be a prayer of simplicity, of *'simple remise à Dieu'* – simply giving yourself wholeheartedly into His hands, to worry, and be troubled and bewildered . . .

I think I was quite bewildered by everything but I knew that somehow I was doing the right thing and I was becoming more and more familiar with the path that leads through darkness, through the cloud. The following quotation appears in my notebook but the source is not given:

> The religious life is their means of sanctification because, as they believe, it is the life to which God calls them – and therefore to follow any other form of life, however they might seem naturally to be suited to it, would be a failure in obedience and therefore in love.

And the following from Bishop Butler's *Prayer: An Adventure in Living*:

> I want God. In fact, there is nothing else I do want absolutely, however many things I find relatively attractive.

These two quotations summed up my feelings at that time and I have tried to keep them before me in all the difficult patches of my development in the monastic life. There were many happy moments in the novitiate: new friendships were formed and much help, support and encouragement were given by the brethren. I began to open up more to others – and to myself – although in some ways this process was cautious and partial.

But there was a lonely side to the novitiate and with it came the awareness that I need companionship. I had always been with people and the deprivation of social life highlighted the need for close friendship which I had taken for granted. The separation from former friends was a great cross, as the value of friendship had been implanted in my heart early in life. The temptation was to look for companionship in the centre of the social life of Belmont, the school; but this was forbidden to novices and with excellent reason. I was given a small job of running the school bookshop on certain afternoons: this was a part of the policy of opening up the novitiate. In some ways it would have been wiser if we had had no contact with the school for at least two or three years. It is easy to rely on props and the possibility of papering over damp patches in the early years of monastic training is likely to produce problems later on. It is important that the monk should experience solitude; adjustment to 'aloneness' and even a certain amount of loneliness is part of the novitiate training. To avoid this by seeking to fill up those times which should be given to prayer, reading, study and silence is to miss the whole point of the monastic life, which is not only to search for God but also to allow ourselves to be found by him. One cannot fully come to terms with oneself in the novitiate or in the early years of monastic life, but one must take the opportunity of the space given in the novitiate and not seek to fill it with work or people.

At the end of my novitiate I was made assistant housemaster in one of the school houses. This was not demanding, but at the end of that academic year, owing to difficult circumstances in the school, I was made housemaster. I was just out of the novitiate and still very green in regard to both the monastic life and the public school system. My previous teaching experience had been within the state system. More troublesome than getting used to the ways of boarders was the difficulty of fitting in one's monastic duties and finding time and peace for prayer in this bewildering new world of school life. I was also made director of music and at the same time expected to do my studies for the priesthood. As I look back on this, it seems an extraordinary burden to have put on someone just out of the novitiate. Somehow I survived and I would attribute my survival partly to the discovery of the charismatic renewal or pentecostal movement, as it was then called.

Our Abbot returned from a conference of English Benedictine Abbots in Oxford in 1971, much taken with the idea of shared prayer, which had been imparted by Prior Luke Rigby of St Louis, USA. He was keen that those interested should begin to pray together and this struck an immediate chord in several of the brethren. We began to share our prayer.

In the informal setting of a prayer group, we learned to pray freely and spontaneously, gradually overcoming our initial embarrassment. We began to be more free in our praise and thanksgiving; we read the Scriptures and shared our insights; we learned to bear one another's burdens and turn them into prayer and, perhaps most important of all, there was space for 'shared silence' when we could listen to the Lord speaking in our hearts.

When talking of 'shared prayer' one must be careful not to give the impression that this form of prayer became more important than the liturgical prayer of the Office which takes place several times each day in the monastic choir. Like personal prayer, shared prayer is nourished by the prayer of the psalms and the reading of the Scriptures which make up the Divine Office. The monk's life revolves around the daily celebration of the Mass and the Divine Office with his brethren and nothing can replace this common prayer. In my Anglican days I had valued the Offices of Matins and Evensong; it seemed natural that Christians should pray together at set times. The daily celebration of the Divine Office was, for me, a great attraction to the Benedictine life. Over the years I grew to know and love the psalms and they became an essential part of my spirituality; their words came readily to my lips during private prayer and in moments of joy and sadness there is always a psalm verse to express our mood and turn it into prayer.

The experience of shared prayer increased my love of the Office. The words of the psalms became more alive and at the same time I began to understand more clearly the meaning of St Benedict's *lectio divina*: not just the study of Holy Scripture but the receiving of God's word, alive and active, in a way that makes our hearts burn within us.

As we grew in shared prayer, we learned more about the renewal movement that had sprung up in the USA. We visited Stanbrook Abbey and prayed and talked with some of the nuns who were also interested. We read books and talked to main-line Pentecostals, and I found in myself a growing thirst for the experience of God which was being talked about under the term 'baptism in the Holy Spirit'. I felt that Christians were getting something from this experience that I was only vaguely grasping but for which I had this strange yearning. I knew that there was more to Christianity than just struggling for virtue and overcoming vice – 'muscular Christianity' with its self-sufficient, almost Pelagian approach – yet I seemed a long way off.

At one prayer gathering at Stanbrook I asked to be prayed over for a new infilling with the Holy Spirit. A Dominican friar from Oxford laid his hands on my head and everyone prayed fervently for this blessing. I did experience a real grace which I couldn't exactly express. It was a change of attitude rather than anything else; there was no rushing wind, but there was calm and peace and a certain 'warmth' in prayer. I began to realize more clearly what was meant by the indwelling Trinity. A more personal approach to God was becoming evident. Something did happen to me in that prayer meeting, but there was more to come: one has to seek the Lord with one's whole heart and hold back nothing from him. A prayer I wrote somewhere around that time expresses the feeling that I had been rather hasty and unprepared the first time I had asked for this grace:

> Make me simple and humble, O Lord. Give me the full blessing of your Spirit not for my own consolation and delight but for your glory, for your Church. Last time, I went wrong, I was too quick, too eager. I looked for an escape from what was around because I was afraid. The Holy Spirit is not an escape but an immersion in reality, in Christ. How could I have been so slow-witted and dull not to realize the effect? I was selfish then and I have realized it, but that was a beginning, even though there has been a lapse, a serious lapse, when I forgot you because there were other things, and although they hurt so much, so very much, yet I preferred them to you because they were easier, more accessible, or seemed to be. God, make me humble, simple, open. Then the Spirit will come in his fullness (if I have faith) as he came on the Twelve and Mary in Jerusalem and they were transformed. I will be transformed, not for my comfort or tranquillity but for your glory and the building up of your Church. Slake my thirst for you, God, living God, living Water, Rock, Manna, life, Light, Love!

I was being brought round to the need for repentance and the admission of my poverty before the Lord: the thirst for living water. I was unprepared, unrepentant, but the Lord brought me to a deeper sense of repentance and of need as I prayed before him when I was on holiday at home in Swansea during Easter week 1972. After reading the Scriptures on the coming of the Holy Spirit in John and Acts, and after a real struggle – a sense of being held back by some power of evil – I prayed in faith to be filled anew with the Holy Spirit and his gifts and at that moment I was filled with joy and prayed and praised in a language I didn't understand.

I still pray in this language with the same sounds, the same conviction of the nearness of God and of the Spirit praying within me, the same ability to start and stop at will and very often with the same sense of joy and peace within. Whatever the gift of tongues may be, whatever this experience of the baptism in the Spirit is, I can only testify to the fact that it is real and that it has a profound effect on people's lives. A few weeks after this experience I wrote in my notebook: 'The great thing about it (tongues) is that in a creature of "ups and downs" like myself, speaking in tongues is a constant reminder of the indwelling Spirit when one is tempted emotionally to think otherwise.'

There are times in prayer when we are unable to express in words our deepest feelings of praise, or our agony, or the needs of ourselves and others. Language is limited on these occasions and there are so few words that really express our deepest feelings. Perhaps it is in this way that one can begin to understand the gift of tongues: an overflow language of incomprehensible sounds which releases that deeper prayer within us that needs to be spoken with the lips if not always understood with the mind. St Paul puts it best when he says:

> Likewise the Spirit helps us in our weakness; for we do not know how to pray as we ought, but the Spirit himself intercedes for us with sighs too deep for words. And he who searches the hearts of men knows what is the mind of the Spirit, because the Spirit intercedes for the saints according to the will of God.

(Rom. 8.26–7, RSV)

God often takes over in our lives at the point of our greatest weakness, when we recognize our inability to cope on our own. This is certainly true in prayer. There is a point when we cannot express with our intellect and language what the heart is crying out to say and I believe that it is at this point that the Spirit can take over and release what would otherwise be shut up in the heart. This release can take the form of an overflow language known as the gift of tongues. It is never easy to explain this gift, but what seems clear from the New Testament and particularly from the First Letter to the Corinthians (chapters 12 and 14) is that it is basically a prayer form: 'For one who speaks in a strange tongue speaks not to men but to God' (1 Cor. 14.2, RSV). It is in this way that most people who have the gift now experience it.

They will testify that it does seem to express the inexpressible. Fr Simon Tugwell, OP, in the second volume of his treatise on prayer, says:

> As the great saints and spiritual writers have all told us, there is a mystery about Christian prayer, such that the one praying will

often not understand much of his own prayer. It is part of our faith, part of our humility, to let God himself pray in us, without always insisting on keeping track with our minds. Although this mysterious dimension of prayer is . . . not confined to praying in tongues, it surely helps us to situate the significance of tongues in our prayer life.

(Simon Tugwell, OP, *Prayer: Keeping Company with God*, Part 2, *Prayer in Practice*, p. 132)

This experience does not change us into saints overnight – far from it! The devil is active and has his victories. Archbishop Temple had this to say about the Holy Spirit:

When we pray 'Come, Holy Ghost, our souls inspire', we had better know what we are about. He will not carry us to easy triumphs and gratifying successes; more probably he will set us some task for God in the full intention that we shall fail, so that others, learning wisdom by our failure, may carry the good cause forward. He may take us through loneliness, desertion by friends, apparent desertion even by God; that was the way Christ went to the Father. He may drive us into the wilderness to be tempted of the devil. He may lead us from the Mount of Transfiguration (if he ever lets us climb it) to the hill that is called the Place of a Skull. For if we invoke him, it must be to help us in doing God's will, not ours. We cannot call upon the

'Creator Spirit, by whose aid
The world's foundations first were laid'

in order to use omnipotence for the supply of our futile pleasures or the success of our futile plans. If we invoke him, we must be ready for the glorious pain of being caught by his power out of our petty orbit into the eternal purposes of the Almighty, in whose onward sweep our lives are as a speck of dust. The soul that is filled with the Spirit must have become purged of all pride or love of ease, all self-complacence and self-reliance; but the soul has found the only real dignity, the only lasting joy. Come then, Great Spirit, come. Convict the world; and convict my timid soul.

(William Temple, *Readings in St John's Gospel*, xvi, vv. 8–11)

I was to discover the truth of these words as the years passed, but certainly at that moment the power of God became real. Soon after this experience came solemn profession, which I approached with confidence, conviction and peace. The three days' retreat following, with fastened hood, were, however, a 'desert' experience when I was tempted to doubt what I had done. God works in strange ways!

Soon after taking solemn vows I relinquished school life for the College of Sant' Anselmo, Rome, and a few years of breathing space in which to do my studies for the priesthood. There were many blessings in Rome. The studies were not difficult but certainly awkward as Italian was the main language used for teaching. The Latin liturgy was a cold-water shock after Belmont's all-vernacular liturgy, but the community at Sant' Anselmo were genuinely kind and friendly and one quickly adapted and made new friends from all over the monastic world. One of the greatest blessings of my stay in Rome was the English-speaking prayer group which met in the Gregorian University every Sunday. Here the deepest and most lasting friendships were made and here I learned many new things in the life of prayer, in the use of Scripture, in praising God and in praying for healing with faith. Here was a group of people made up of priests, sisters, clerical students and laity who were totally committed to the Kingdom of God. We were anxious to express this in spontaneous worship and sharing with each other the goodness and love of God towards us, together with our fears, doubts and weaknesses. We found mutual support and encouragement in so doing. I made several close friends in this group, but one especially has been a great support to me over the last few years, Dr Bill Hood, an art historian who teaches in Oberlin, Ohio. His insight and sense of humour have helped me put many things in perspective in both my spiritual and my monastic life.

After Rome came my ordination to the priesthood in September 1974. The moment to which I had looked forward for so many years was presided over by Bishop Donal Mullins who had been assistant chaplain and fellow student in university days, and it was an added pleasure to have the words of anointing spoken by him in Welsh. One cannot even begin to comprehend the great mystery of the priesthood; one can only minister in Christ's name and in the power of his Spirit, always conscious of God's great love despite one's personal unworthiness.

I returned to the school as housemaster of the same house and was again in charge of music. For a year or so everything went well, but I was continually aware of the same pitfalls as before: over-involvement in things temporal to the detriment of things eternal, something which our English Benedictine Constitutions are most anxious to prevent in the life of our monks.

On New Year's Day 1976 my stepmother, Kit, died suddenly after a brain haemorrhage. Kit's sudden death left my father heartbroken. The trauma of the situation hit me hard and deep. I was an only child, so what was I to do with my father, who needed my support at this time? Although his health was poor, I could not leave the monastery and the work I was doing to look after him, yet I sensed his anxiety at being alone again. Time is the only healer in such situations and he slowly recovered his balance, but eighteen months later his diseased lungs could hold out no longer and I was with him at his death, which came quickly and peacefully. This was the first time I had been with someone at the moment of dying and the simplicity of my father's passing filled me with peace and did much to heal my own fear of death.

But immediately after Kit's death I was anything but peaceful. I became anxious for my father, depressed and insomniac; I seemed unable to share my problems with anyone. I was beset with guilt and fear and could barely cope with my work. When I could go on no longer, when the heavens seemed shut tight and God obviously was not going to take away my troubles miraculously, I had to forget my pride and open myself to that healing love of Christ which can only come to us through the compassion of our brethren. I found sympathy and understanding in my Abbot, in the brethren and in my doctor, and gradually I was restored and refashioned. But I had learned to trust others; learned that my brethren can love me despite my faults just as the Lord loves us, that I had to accept myself, that I had to give myself to others and be dependent on others. These lessons are often hard to learn: it's one thing to ask the Holy Spirit: 'Melt me, mould me, fill me, use me', but another thing to go through the experience of being melted and moulded. Often the Lord allows us to experience this incredible tunnel of darkness and isolation to enable us to have greater empathy with those who suffer in a similar way and to be a channel of his peace to them. To live with Christ means to die with Christ, but it can be a painful experience. The hell of isolation and near-despair is a modern-day sickness, and into this we must carry the love of the Father, the peace, salvation and healing of Jesus and the balm of the Holy Spirit.

I still feel my fragility in that experience of darkness and I still feel the need for deeper healing. I can see the obstacles that I myself put up to that healing process: my selfishness, cowardice, sensuality, pride and especially my lack of prayer and my half-givenness. The Lord Jesus is there waiting, giving, loving and it is only our blindness and hard-heartedness that prevent the flow of his grace. He wants us to experience the freedom of the children of God; we are sometimes too timid to enter into this freedom, for we tend to lurk in the shadows instead of getting out and playing in the sunshine of God's love. We have yet to experience in ourselves those words of St John: 'Perfect love casts out fear.' I continually ask myself why I don't enter more fully into this freedom, this perfect love, and the same answer forms in my heart: lack of trust, lack of love, lack of prayer.

I have always before my mind St Thérèse's picture of the little child who gets separated from its father in a crowd. Then suddenly they spot each other and the child runs to the father, who gathers the child up into his arms and hugs it to himself. In that instant the child is secure and free from fear. We seem unable to let go of things, of ourselves, our fears, our sins, our past and so on and to resign ourselves totally to the everlasting arms of God. John Powell says this in his spiritual autobiography:

> Open all the doors and windows of your soul to the Lord. Don't keep any rooms locked or closed off to him. Let Jesus take over. The depth of the faith that releases the power of God is measured by your own willingness to let God direct your life. Raise yourself up to him as a gift. Surrender your life and your heart to him.

> (John Powell, SJ, *He Touched Me: My Pilgrimage of Prayer*, p. 48)

The Holy Spirit leads us towards the Father in the same way as Jesus was led. We need to be conformed to the Father's will, and this he does bit by bit, sometimes gently, sometimes more forcefully, but all the time leading us from the isolation of self to the truth of God's love and his presence within each of us.

This is where I find myself now: still very much on pilgrimage and searching continually. I am sometimes confused about the work I have to do and feel inadequate to meet its demands, still holding the reins lightly in my hands in case I should be asked to hand over to someone else. Very often I am beset with weakness, temptation and failure to love God and others and myself. Yet somehow, in a strange, mysterious way, I know that God, the object of our searching, is taking the initiative and providing the means of grace and the strength of the Spirit to enable us to respond. From this realization springs perseverance, deep joy, praise and thanksgiving for being among those whom he has called to seek his face.

Father, you have always been there, even from my earliest years, gently leading me on. Just as you were present in the time of the Exodus, a pillar of cloud by day and a pillar of fire by night, leading the Hebrew people out of bondage into freedom, so it is with me. You have always been there, Lord, leading me out of darkness into your own wonderful light; from ignorance into truth; from the isolation of self into the community of love.

Despite my wanderings, despite my complaining, despite my unwillingness to go forward, you have never deserted me. You have always remained faithful in the midst of my infidelity.

In the daytime of my joy, your hidden brightness, the wisdom of the Holy Spirit, has gone before me and drawn me after it; in the night-time of my isolation, despondency and fear, your pillar of fire, the refining Spirit, has been there working in my heart, thawing my iciness and purifying me. Who can resist you, great God, ever seeking after us and compelling us to run to the light of your truth and the warmth of your love?

But, Father, pilgrim that I am, I still wander into the byways of pride, self-pity and fear. I take my eyes off the goal all too often. I allow my weariness to lessen my response to your infinite love. Forgive me as I turn my eyes back to you. Sharpen my awareness of Your Son, Jesus, my Brother, who takes me by the hand and pulls me along in my reluctance. Too often have I looked back over my shoulder, forgetful of your infinite desire to lead me on to the glory that lies ahead.

Lord God, how thankful I am that you are continually searching for me; how thankful I am that your grace prompts me to recognize you and to give myself to you even in my imperfect way. Lord Jesus, how thankful I am that your love, stronger than death, will never let me go. Holy Spirit, sweep me up into this love which unites you and the Father and the Son; let it flow into me and overflow from me to all whom I meet. Let it lighten their darkness and increase their joy. Let it draw me into unity with my brethren and with all those whom I serve and will serve in your name until the end of my days.

Glory and praise to you, Father, Son and Holy Spirit, for ever. Amen.

A Spiritual Jigsaw

DOM DAVID MORLAND

I was born at Winchester on 25 January 1943 and known, I believe, as Caruso in the local nursing home. I only just managed to get born in England rather than on the high seas or in the Far East, as my parents returned from Japan in the autumn of 1942 where they had been interned (and well treated) by the Japanese for nine months after Pearl Harbor. My three elder brothers were all born in the Far East, two in Japan and one in China. In fact we had close diplomatic and Far Eastern connections, since my maternal grandfather was British Ambassador in Japan in the 1930s: my father was his private secretary and so met, and married, my mother. Thirty years later he followed in his father-in-law's footsteps and ended his diplomatic career in the same post. Both my parents had a great love and knowledge of Japan and my father spoke and wrote the language fluently. It was used on occasion between them when they did not want the children to understand what was being said. This diplomatic background meant that from early childhood I had the feeling of living in an international world with personal connections from all over the globe and particularly in the Far East.

I was baptized twice, a blessing which has no doubt stood me in good stead later in life. The reason was that my mother, not wishing her children possibly to end up in limbo if we were accidently dropped on the head by a careless nurse, baptized us herself as soon as she had a moment to herself after we were born, using water from the glass thoughtfully left by the midwife. Not wishing to cause unnecessary ecclesiastical disturbance, she did not bother to mention this private rite to the local clergy and so we were all christened later in more conventional fashion.

My father and mother had entirely different characters and were admirably suited to each other, one complementing the other in a remarkable way. My mother, as the above incident illustrates, is ebullient, outgoing, and forthright, quite irrepressible and entirely unconcerned about public opinion, sometimes to the embarrassment of her husband or children. She is generous-hearted and utterly determined. Her faith is simple, certain and extremely powerful. She believes in miracles and often seems to obtain them: she treats the Almighty rather like a shop assistant, with great courtesy and complete confidence that she will get what she wants. It is an attitude to life which she does not restrict to the sphere of the divine. Examples of her unconventional determination are legion and one will have to suffice. In the 1930s she travelled back with three friends from the Far East on the Trans-Siberian Railway. The trains were fairly primitive and rather dirty and my mother objected to the fact that she could not have her regular bath on the twelve-day journey. Undeterred by her almost entire ignorance of Russian she went up to the engine driver and managed to persuade him to rig up a pump and some hot water. So every morning she proceeded down the train in her dressing gown and took her bath with water from the tender while the engine driver modestly gazed out over the Russian steppes.

My father's temperament and personality were entirely different. He was brought up as a Quaker and became a Catholic when he was at Cambridge. He was intelligent, reserved and deeply religious, with an excellent sense of humour and a total lack of diplomatic guile or pomposity. His Quaker roots gave him a great sense of truth and justice, qualities which I think he did not always find in the Catholic Church in the same measure. There was quiet strength and depth about him which commanded enormous respect among colleagues and friends. In the family, although my mother seemed the more forthright and commanding of the two, there was never any doubt where final authority lay. My parents were entirely dedicated to each other and it was a marriage of rare devotion, happiness and affection.

We were blessed with vast numbers of relations, mostly on my mother's side: she rejoiced in forty-six first cousins, mostly of the Scottish Fraser clan. Many of them were richer and grander than us and had large houses where we stayed as children when my parents were abroad, and were always made to feel very much at home. Despite these parental absences we have always been a very close-knit family and this has continued now that my brothers are married and have children of their own. My mother always wanted a larger family: four seemed very meagre. In particular she wanted a daughter and I believe I was due to be called Carolyn but it did not turn out that way.

I had a very happy childhood mostly in Alresford, Hampshire, where my parents bought a house in 1945 to be near my grandparents and other cousins who lived nearby. In fact my first conscious memory is of moving into Wykeham House when I was two years old. I can still see the shape of the hall as it was when I perched half-way up the stairs while the furniture was being carted in. Before that, my father had been working at Bletchley, helping to decipher Japanese codes. Immediately after the end of the Japanese war my father returned to Japan with the first British mission, my mother following a few months later after a gigantic tussle with the Foreign Office who did not think conditions were suitable for wives. It took her and a friend daily visits to the Foreign Office for three weeks to persuade the ever more exasperated officials to see otherwise.

We had a wonderful nanny called Dixie, who came from Stoke-on-Trent. She was devoted to the children and would not even go away on holiday without taking one of us with her. If she was faced with any difficult question to which she did not know the answer, she would invariably reply: 'Wait and see, as Asquith says.' She was also full of the imperial spirit. On one occasion, when war was looming, one of the Japanese servants rather apologetically informed my father that he would have to leave to join the army. On saying goodbye to Dixie he received the withering comment: 'You silly man, you know we always win our wars!' As a child my love was equally divided between my mother and Dixie. I can recall at about the age of six asking myself whether I loved my mother or Dixie more and deciding that I could not make up my mind. When Dixie died after my first term at prep school, after struggling silently and selflessly with cancer for some time before that, it left a gap in my life which took a long time to fill. From both her and my parents I received a basic sense of what was really important in life: not power or money or prestige, but affection, kindness, honesty, justice, faith and prayer.

Both my parents were devoted and faithful Catholics, though by no means overawed by the clergy. My father went to Mass every day and they both had a deep personal faith, a simple sense of the reality and love of God. This was reinforced by a remarkable event that occurred in the mid-1950s. My father had for some time been suffering from a serious blood disease which the doctors were unable to cure and he was in danger of being invalided out of the Foreign Office. Apart from anything else this would have been catastrophic financially as the four of us were still at school or university. In desperation my mother asked one of the Ampleforth monks who was a friend of hers to bring down the hand of Nicholas Postgate (a local Yorkshire priest martyred during penal times) which is kept at Ampleforth. I can well remember Fr Peter Utley turning up at Wykeham House in an old shooting brake carrying the sacred relic. I think that once all were assembled, no one knew quite what to do. Anyway, some ceremony of blessing and prayers took place and Father Peter returned to Ampleforth to restore the relic to the Abbot. On the next visit to the doctors my father's blood disease was gone.

It was a considerable wrench to leave home and the secure happiness of childhood to go to Gilling Castle, the preparatory school of Ampleforth College. The reason I went to Ampleforth was that in the 1930s, when Ampleforth College was beginning to prosper, the word went round the Catholic mafia of my mother's relations that this was the place to support and so all four of us were educated there. For my first two years at Gilling I was pretty miserable, though I don't think I ever mentioned the fact to anyone, but after that things began to look up and on the whole I enjoyed my days at school. I was successful academically and made a good number of friends, some of whom I still keep up with. On reaching the upper school I found myself one of thirty-three new entrants to a house which was being started that year. This was great fun as it meant that we had no one above us to boss us around and could make our own traditions and history. It was a varied and gifted group, intellectually and in other ways, and no less than seven tried their religious vocation, mostly in the monastery at Ampleforth.

I do not remember when I first began to think of becoming a monk. I think it was when I was about sixteen or seventeen. I was certainly influenced by the kindness, dedication and prayerfulness of my housemaster. There were also one or two other monks who operated in a more freelance way around the school whom I got to know very well. With one in particular I remember having long talks late into the night about God, life, human relationships and more or less everything else. This certainly made a difference to me. Then there was a growing sense of the value of a community dedicated to a way of life and an ideal which was based on faith and at the same time quite matter-of-fact and human. I also recall one school retreat when I first tried reading *The Cloud of Unknowing*. Even though it was an immature experience (I did not know myself well enough to be able to encounter 'the cloud of unknowing' with anything more than a superficial contact) there was something genuine there which I have never lost: the sense of the mystery of God and that prayer is not so much a matter of words or ideas but rather a deep, inarticulate longing for one in whom one's whole being can rest and be at peace. It is to do with leaving a space in which the silence of God can become real. Even then I struggled to empty my mind and heart so that there could be a still point of desire and of 'knowing' which the mystery of God could fill and expand. It is a question of getting out of the way and letting God take over.

I remember too a surprisingly clear and logical insight that if there was a God and Christianity was true, then it was fundamentally worth while keeping the reality of God the main priority of one's life. I was sufficiently self-aware to realize that I could not do that on my own and that I needed the disciplined framework of community life whose *raison d'être* was the service of God. If I pursued an ordinary career in the world it was unlikely that this insight would remain real and active. I knew that monastic life would be hard but somehow it was what I began to want, something to which I was drawn as though by a magnet, by a quiet and persistent voice which I could not ignore. Somehow this corresponded to a self which would not be happy with anything but the absolute of God. I do not think I ever seriously considered trying any other religious order or the secular priesthood. I suppose that was mostly a matter of youth and the lack of other experience. I do not even recall consciously thinking much about becoming a monk of the Order of St Benedict: it was more a question of being drawn to do what these people were doing and to try their way of life. I recall at my first interview with Abbot Herbert Byrne, while I was still a boy in the school, being hard pressed to find a reason I could put into words for wanting to join the monastery. I think I said something rather vague about wishing to be part of a group with a common outlook and aim, to which his somewhat tart and, as I later discovered, utterly characteristic reply was, 'Er, you might say the same about the Soviet Praesidium!'

I was not especially pious as a boy although there was quite a strong and matter-of-fact religious atmosphere in the school at that time and particularly in my house, so that daily Mass and regular confession were not regarded as especially odd or burdensome. When I left the school in December 1960 I had not made up my mind whether to ask to join the novitiate the following September or to go up to Cambridge. There had never been any pressure from any of the monks to become a member of the community. There was quiet support and encouragement and advice when asked for but no overt pressure. My parents, whom I had rather shyly told about a year earlier, were both glad, although my mother thought it would be more sensible to go to university first.

On leaving school I went to Italy for several months where I stayed with a wonderful elderly couple called de Bylandt: he was the Dutch Ambassador in Rome and she was an Italian from Florence. He was the perfect European, intelligent, courteous and cultured; she was outspoken, generous and extremely ugly in a somehow distinguished and attractive way. As well as the Embassy in Rome they had a house in Tuscany, at Impruneta near Florence, a most beautiful place set amidst olive groves, vineyards and cypress trees. I spent quite a lot of time up there and grew to love it deeply. While in Rome I decided a good way to see the city would be to go to all the stational churches during Lent. Pope John had recently decided to make more of the forty stational churches so there was usually some cardinal there to celebrate Mass and lead a procession through the streets. They were very Italian occasions: colourful, chaotic and yet strangely moving and genuine. But I think it was at Impruneta at the Easter of 1961 that I finally decided to ask to join the novitiate that year rather than go up to Cambridge. I do not recall any definite new insight, still less a blinding revelation: it was rather a matter of things falling quietly into place. It became clear that despite any fears I might have this was the right thing to do, the thing that deep down I was drawn to. I do not know whether I said anything much about it to Willem and Emy, my host and hostess. They were very close and had almost adopted me, being childless themselves, while my parents were abroad in Japan, but I was very shy and wary about saying anything to anyone about my intentions, in characteristic adolescent fashion. In May of that year I went off on my own to Greece. I had intended to go with my cousin Rosemary, who was in Rome at the time, but this suggestion was vetoed by her mother. *Autres temps, autres moeurs*. The trip to Greece was very enlightening, not only scenically and culturally but also emotionally and personally, since it was the first time I had been entirely on my own for any length of time. Sometimes I felt enormously lonely, sometimes exhilarated and open to anything. There were numerous amusing incidents: on one occasion I was guided up a mountain in Corfu by a crowd of Greek schoolchildren and on our return to the local village was presented by a young girl with a rose and a bean which were handed to me with a shy smile. I did not know what to do with the bean so I ate it to the great amusement of all. On my return I went to Naples where I met my parents who had just returned by ship from Japan. The last couple of months were spent at home at Alresford in a mood of some trepidation about what life would be like in the monastery. As it turned out it was quite different from anything I had anticipated, both much richer and much more painful than I could have imagined.

I entered the novitiate at Ampleforth in September 1961 with fifteen other novices, the largest group the Abbey had ever taken at one time. This happened just a week after the consecration of the new Abbey Church. Perhaps it was a sort of blessing on the faith and generosity of the community and its friends which had made the building of the church possible. On the whole I found the novitiate a pretty shattering experience. This was not the fault of my fellow novices who were friendly and congenial, nor of the novice master, an excellent and holy Irishman who was strong on Scripture and weak on organization, and a very shrewd and sympathetic judge of people. It was shattering because it exposed me to myself, forcing me inwards because of the lack of external satisfaction. There were almost no activities in which I could shine. I can remember looking forward each week to the Latin hymns class, given by Abbot Herbert Byrne, simply because I was the only one who could translate them and it gave me a chance to shine. I realized how inadequate and superficial this was. There was a forced interiority which made me aware of my own weaknesses, the extent to which I had depended on external success and stimuli, the darker side of my reasons for wishing to become a monk: fear of sex and the world and a desire for security and a clear path in life which would not involve personal decision. Looking back on it now twenty years later I can see many reasons why it would have been better to go up to Cambridge first and gain more experience and independence. And yet I am not sure that I was not right all the same to go straight in: there is sometimes a moment when one can take a particular decision which affects one's whole life and this is a moment of grace which it is important to lay hold of and follow through with a definite decision. The ways of God are strange indeed and even one's fears and weaknesses can be used to lead one in the way that God wills one to take. In time they are both revealed and healed, but it is true that the first discovery of the darker side of one's nature and motivation is very painful and humiliating. I can remember writing to my father during a particularly difficult patch towards the end of the first year in the novitiate to tell him of some of my misgivings and new-found self-knowledge. He wrote back a marvellous letter full of sane and wise advice, the gist of which was that whatever one's motives for having started on something the important thing was to see whether it was the right thing for one in itself. If that were the case then gradually one's reasons and motives would be purified and transformed.

Not all the novitiate was bleak by any means. There were moments of relief and even high comedy. With sixteen of us in the novitiate the mood was lively and colourful. About half-way through the first year many of us were seized with fits of uncontrollable giggles, probably a safety valve to relieve nervous tension. These usually occurred, as is the way with this sort of laughter, at the most unsuitable times, especially in choir in the solemn silence after Compline, the last Office of the day. Sometimes the whole front bench of the choirstalls would literally be shaking from the barely suppressed mirth of the inmates. After a while the prior got exasperated with our performance and told those who were particularly vociferous to kneel out in the middle of choir. This, however, was disastrous as, far from reducing the level of giggles, it merely transferred their physical location, so that sometimes one could see up to half a dozen prostrate forms doubled up with mirth on the floor like lunatic frogs. Another source of enjoyment during the novitiate was getting to know the local countryside round Ampleforth. Even though we had been in the school, a great deal of the moors and woods and valleys was quite unknown and we used to go on energetic runs led by an ex-paratroop captain, which ended in the summer in bathes in the nearby river Rye.

The round of activities in the novitiate was quite restricted: the study of the Rule of St Benedict, the psalms and other parts of the Bible, sacristy work and manual labour. The last I found rather irksome, not being practical by nature. I can remember one July afternoon weeding the cemetery garden in the wood behind the monastery when I felt especially gloomy. I decided that if things did not look up in a week I would leave, even though I was full of fears about facing the outside world and seeming to have failed in what I had undertaken. After a week the mood had not changed and yet I stayed. That moment of decision has always been for me evidence of the reality of God and the truth of a personal vocation. It was forged with such pain that I could not believe it was self-deception or illusion. It was a moment of revelation, a discovery that in the will of God lay peace and that in suffering came the growth of a desire for God in himself. This was not a matter of evident personal fulfilment but rather of truth. The real self responded to a call even though the following of it would certainly involve sacrifice and suffering. For me the novitiate was an extreme case of the abandonment of human fulfilment, of the sacrifice of everything for the sake of God. I began to glimpse that God is indeed a jealous lover and will brook no rivals: the whole world is in a way turned grey so as not to be a false god tempting one to leave the right path. One is rather like a barnacle clinging to a rock under water: gradually the shell is prised from the surface of the rock so that it can float free in the sea and be carried by the current of God's will. But it is a painful and costly process, for there are so many hidden attachments which have one by one to be detached from the rock. So I took simple vows after one year with a basic certainty that this was right, that this was what I wanted to do, but with little expectation of enjoying anything again. In fact I did enjoy things then and still more later, but there was a real abandonment of future success or satisfaction.

After two years in the novitiate and a year in the broader life of the whole community, which entailed a small amount of contact with the school (I became quite good at refereeing rugger games), I went up to St Benet's Hall, the Ampleforth house of studies at Oxford, to study Mods and Greats. There new horizons opened out: I much enjoyed the intellectual stimulus, especially philosophy under the penetrating if eccentric tutelage of Elizabeth Anscombe. I made a lot of friends, both men and women, and began to relax, especially in the company of the latter. I think I benefited from being rather older than my contemporaries: relations with dons were easier and more mature as one was less likely to treat them as schoolmasters and more as tutors who could also become friends. Life in the Hall was lively and warm with a lot of young monks and a new Master, Fr James Forbes, who toned down somewhat the austerities of the previous regime and certainly improved the food. At one time we had an ex-chef from the *Queen Elizabeth* whose culinary skill seemed to improve with the consumption of alcohol. Guest nights were memorable affairs with Charles arrayed in a chef's hat, a more or less white coat and filthy trousers.

There was, however, another side to my life while I was at Oxford. I felt a very considerable tension between prayer and the rest of life. I was convinced that to pray, especially when I was back in Ampleforth during the holidays, was the only thing worth doing and I would spend long hours just meditating. At the same time I felt guilty because I thought I should be doing other things, especially work. But somehow there was a desire to pray which commanded my obedience at a deeper level. In time a better balance was achieved between prayer, people and work but at the time it was a painful experience.

There was also a tension between letting go, trusting in God, and the desire for achievement and self-justification; for a way of life that would be holy, morally good and give me a peace of mind which would eradicate guilt. Yet I was aware that I could not achieve self-justification. I remember a short period during Lent one year when I tried such a model life, trying to be observant and do everything correctly, to love people and to do my work properly. By Easter the whole thing had collapsed and I vowed never again to follow the law in that sort of way. I was at an extreme of interiority where the externals, whether of activity or of people, were devalued. I thought that I could discover and respond to God on my own with an interiority disconnected from the world and other people. This was a mistake but perhaps something it was necessary to go through to find one pole of the search for wholeness and for it to become very real. In general I feel that growth is a zigzag course, a spiral rather than an orderly procession of stages, and that no part of the zig-zag can be avoided. It is not necessarily wrong to go to extremes as long as one does not fall off the edge. The divine gravity does draw one back into the centre. Although I am unable now to evisage interiority or union with God in the same way as I did then, the experience provided a sort of sediment of truth which was of value later.

After one year at Oxford, in September 1965, I took solemn vows. The year away from Ampleforth was a valuable test of my real desire to stay as a monk, as it gave me more adult and varied experience against which to measure my monastic intentions. At the time the Second Vatican Council was just drawing to a close and I realized that a permanent commitment to a monastic community had to take a different form from that of an earlier and more stable period, even though the heart of the matter – obedience, stability and conversion of life, the Benedictine vows – remained the same. The difference lay in the changes one could both see and anticipate in the Church and the world in which the vows were being made. The unknown character of the future and the likelihood of quite radical change both in the life of the individual and the nature of the community were much more evident. One could not believe that the community itself and one's own personal path in it would form a measured and tranquil rhythm which could be predicted from past patterns. This meant a particular emphasis on the vow of conversion of life, a concentration on the basic elements of the life rather than on the external fabric. It meant too that one was throwing in one's lot with a given group of people and their history and future, for richer, for poorer, in sickness and in health. One could not predict how that would work out. It was clear that there would be much change; it was also probable that there would be many obstacles to the sort of development which one might believe oneself was right, though just how burdensome that fact was to be was mercifully hidden at the time. In my own case I am glad that some of this was apparent when I took solemn vows and was deliberately borne in mind as I came to that decision. It meant that fidelity to one's vows and to the community, whatever the difficulties both in oneself and in others or the institution, was of paramount importance and was always worth while since it was written into one's solemn promise and therefore had the assurance of divine blessing and assistance. I think without that awareness some of the doubts and difficulties of the following years would have been very hard to bear. It has struck me since what a precious quality faithfulness is, the ability to go on trusting in the guidance and help of God and to hold firm to one's commitment of stability in a community and way of life, especially in a time of change when many landmarks disappear and one's faith in God's overarching providence has to be purified like gold in a furnace. There is a strong temptation when things get difficult to rewrite one's autobiography in order to justify abandoning one's promises. I do not say that in all cases this is what happens, but I am grateful myself that right from the beginning I did have some glimmering of the cost that fidelity would entail, which meant that later I could not say to myself that I did not know what I was taking on when I made solemn vows.

The ceremony of solemn vows is a moving and impressive occasion. Quite a lot of the time one is face downwards on a black pall in the middle of the choir while one's brethren sing the litany of the saints. The whole liturgy is centred on the mystery of death and resurrection, a total surrender of oneself and one's life into God's hands in the concrete circumstances of a particular community and its way of life. At one point those just professed sing: *Suscipe me, Domine, secundum eloquium tuum, et vivam, et non confundas me ab exspectatione mea* ('If you uphold me by your promise I shall live; let my hopes not be in vain') (Ps. 118 (119).116). It is sung three times to a haunting plainchant melody on an ever higher note and somehow it captures the yearning and the affliction and the trust of a soul whose life is to be handed over to the following of Christ, one who is somehow certain that his hopes will not be confounded because God has bound himself in a solemn promise to guard and protect and lead to eternal life.

After the profession ceremony there is a custom that the newly professed are in total silence for three days with their hoods up, only to be taken down for the reception of Communion at Mass. This is rather hard on family and friends who have come up for the occasion but it is meant to symbolize the passage from death to new life in imitation of Christ's three days in the tomb. For me it was a magical time. There is a wood behind the monastery on a

steeply sloping hill with terraces wrought out of the hill by
industrious Victorian predecessors. It looks out over the valley
and is a beautiful spot. I spent many hours up there after solemn
vows just bathing in a great sense of peace and homecoming. All
the struggle was worth it: whatever was to happen in the future I
just knew in my heart and mind and bones that it was all right and
that God wanted me simply to be there. In later years the memory
of this moment was a great consolation, a sort of guarantee that
the path I was on was the right one.

In the summer of 1968 I took finals at Oxford and was rather put
out not to get a First, especially as I had had to travel down from
the north of Scotland, where I was on holiday, for two half-hour
vivas. I had been warned that the presiding examiner for
philosophy was against giving Firsts except to brilliant candi-
dates, but even so, being pipped at the post rankled at the time. I
remember later receiving some solace from Elizabeth Anscombe,
who pointed out that if you got a Double First you were marked
for life, by yourself as well as others, while if you didn't you
valued the actual education you had received rather than the
degree.

After finishing at Oxford I started theology in preparation for
ordination. At the time there were a number of Ampleforth
monks studying at Fribourg University in Switzerland, a
tradition begun by Abbot Basil Hume and others who went there
just after the Second World War. But Abbot Basil decided it was
worth trying other places and told me to look round for
alternatives. In the end we fixed on Munich, which had a good
theology faculty, a suitable hall of residence run by the
Benedictine monastery of Ettal and the presence of one English
monk who had started a year earlier. On arrival I did not know
much German, having only done O levels years before, but I am
fortunate in being able to pick up languages quickly and in six
months I became reasonably fluent. It was quite a change after
Oxford: instead of cosy tutorials there were massive lecture halls
and the royal presence of Herr Professor who was usually
friendly but distant. A good deal of red tape seemed to afflict the
institution and even student protest movements, much in
evidence in 1968, seemed to require secretaries, minutes and
elaborate organization. But the standard of theology was high
and I learned a great deal, especially in the study of Scripture and
dogmatic theology. Munich too was a wonderful place with
operas, concerts, theatres, delicious beer and wine and easy
access to the Bavarian Alps and the marvellous baroque churches
and palaces of the area. I made a great number of new friends and

did a good deal of travelling, including a month in Paris in the spring of 1969 and a week in Prague later in the same year. In retrospect I can see just how free a rein I was given by the Abbot, though I don't know that I appreciated it at the time.

In some ways, however, it was a difficult time. There was a ferment of questioning in the Church and nowhere more intense than in the theology faculties of German universities. Many priests and Religious were leaving their ministry or orders and naturally many of their criticisms and hopes became my own. The world of Ampleforth, its public school and relatively conservative monastic tradition, seemed very remote and even alien at times, when one was discussing radical change in politics or theology in a Munich Weinkeller. I found that pressure quite considerable upon myself. It was so easy to reinterpret my own past or write a new biography where I could trace my motivation in joining the monastery to adolescent insecurity, to fear of sex or of the world, and to come to doubt whether I was really in the right place.

This meant that on returning to Ampleforth I felt somehow out of place and it was not easy to find people with whom I could share my doubts and questions about the community and its future. At this time a large new building programme was started in the school, which, given the logic of continuing this type of work and the nature of the community, was a perfectly reasonable thing to do. But I, and some others, felt that this was a reversal of priorities and that we were missing the opportunity for a more searching examination of the role and future of a Benedictine monastery in a post-Second Vatican Council Church. I felt myself quite a stranger at home at Conventual Chapters where these decisions were being taken. Perhaps I should have spoken out more, not so much because there was something of value to say but rather because by not doing so I felt more alienated. In fact there was probably a more sympathetic and open audience than I would have given the community credit for. I think I was rather too idealistic and intellectual about it, without sufficient sensitivity to the actual needs of the majority of the people in the community and the real limits of possible change, but nevertheless the questions were real ones and I felt there was a lack of adequate discussion of basic issues. This brought about a tension between personal integrity and loyalty; between the following of a truth wherever it would lead and the commitment of stability to a particular community with its history and future.

On the other hand, by being away and by visiting other monasteries, I did come to a greater appreciation of many of the strengths of my own community which I had rather taken for granted before: its sanity and wisdom, the goodness and variety of the people in it, the humanity and kindness of its superiors, Abbot Basil in particular. Whatever the problems, Ampleforth did remain home and I never seriously wanted to be a monk of any other house.

After two years in Munich I moved to Rome, to study at the Benedictine college of Sant' Anselmo. This was one of the happiest times of my life. I love Italy and all things Italian. Rome is almost my favourite city, with its tortuous back streets, its yellow stucco walls, the multiplicity of churches and fountains and squares, the way it is a palimpsest of European history, each level flung higgledy-piggledy upon the next with a random and careless beauty which is the more poignant for being often decaying and unkempt. The regime at Sant' Anselmo was remarkably liberal with an excellent American Abbot in charge, and the variety of people and experience I found a real tonic. The theology was mostly in the German style as the professors hailed in large measure from German-speaking areas, so I found reasonable continuity with my studies in Munich. The international mix in the college was fascinating and the variety of monastic traditions and outlooks at times bewildering. On the whole it reinforced my regard for the English Benedictine version. While I was in Rome I travelled a good deal round Italy, including one glorious week in Sicily in the winter of 1970 with three other monks from various parts of the world and an artist called Pat Hakim, half English and half Pakistani, whom I knew well in Rome. Ever since, when I try to envisage heaven, I feel like calling it Sicilian time, in memory of those golden days in Sicily.

One thread running through that period was a consequence of the philosophical training I received at Oxford, particularly the emphasis on the empirical, upon meaning being found in a shared language of a community: a certain scepticism about the authenticity of a private language or interior experience. In conjunction with this, my rediscovery of the 'human' made me much more doubtful about the extreme pole of interiority which had been such a reality at an earlier period. I began to feel that the truth about God and about man had to be worked out in the ebb and flow of a whole world of people, human relationships and politics, as well as mysticism. I became much more socially critical and more concerned with justice in the world. The whole area of social, economic and political structures became something I felt much more deeply. I experienced a certain tension between the monastic ideal and the demands of active engagement in the

81

world's problems. I became more concerned to trace the connection between the sort of critique represented by the monastic tradition and the critique of society which one might find in Marxist writings or in the growing schools of political or liberation theologians.

At this time I had a growing sense that we were living in a new world. Many of the assumptions underlying existing institutions, whether in the Church or in the world, were unable to cope with the critical state of the Church or society. This was a judgement upon a traditional institution or monastic community, one which summoned it to purify itself and discover a new heart which would be less attached to the various vested interests which had proved their value in the past but might not be so relevant in the future. It was not a question of declaring modernity to be a new god. On the contrary, many of the traditional patterns of wisdom in the Benedictine Community reaching back over centuries could offer a critique and a positive outcome to many of the problems which face man today. Among the signs of the times were a search for new forms of community, a desire for experience of the transcendent, a desire for the integration of the intellectual and a simpler way of life, the realization that the system and sheer size of institutions could itself be alienating and destructive. In consequence there was recognition of the value of an autonomous group of people, working out their own destiny.

However, that traditional wisdom can easily be overlaid with demands of a more recent past, so that the task of renewal in a large and ancient institution is very difficult. The insights or vision which seemed so obvious to me could not easily be communicated. They did not always receive an open or willing audience. Now I can see that much of that was my own arrogance and conviction of rightness, not simply the blindness or obtuseness of others. Nevertheless there was truth in that insight and I began to feel towards the end of my time abroad that there was a great need in my own community for experimental groups which would not necessarily be tied to the demands of keeping the show on the road, but would have a greater freedom and flexibility and perhaps a clearer vision and a more evident order of priorities in their practical life. At the same time I was aware that to get something of this sort off the ground would not be at all easy.

Another area of that sense of newness was to do with religious language and paths of spirituality. I found it increasingly difficult to read the Fathers or medieval writers in such a way that I could appropriate their message and insights about God, prayer and the path of holiness. At the same time the Scriptures, the New Testament in particular, became more and more important. They seemed to provide a well-spring of truth which in the light of modern scriptural research could often have a very deep significance for us. The figure of Jesus became more mysterious: demanding and questioning as well as consoling. The history of that man as the revelation of the meaning of God and of the human story took on a significance which it had not possessed before. Yet the gap between that mysterious incarnation of God and the present state of the institutional Church and of religious communities within it became much greater. They, and I as a member of them, came as much under the judgement of God as under his promises. I looked through other disciplines: psychology and other religions, political philosophy and other areas of the human sciences in order to find new coinage in which to cash out the current religious language of spirituality. It was not only a theoretical concern. I have always felt a deep emotional need for truth. Ideas and concepts are not just abstract, irrelevant or superficial; they involve me and they demand that I work through them and try to find the clearest, most accurate and genuine language to rediscover the mystery of faith. The gap between Jesus – who he is and what he demands – and the contemporary state of the Church had also a more practical bearing. I found it hard to identify myself with the pattern of holiness which I could see embodied in older monks. I could respect and learn but not imitate. That was quite painful because I could see the need for spiritual guidance, some sort of guru in order to find direction.

I doubted whether anyone else could really understand; whether they were, in a sense, trustworthy. Not that they were untrustworthy, but rather that they could not point out for me the right signals, the right landmarks and direction. Again, looking back on that, I think there was a good deal of arrogance, a sense of being someone special, living in a new age. Even though a pattern of holiness is obviously not generalizable and may take on a new shape and form in a different period, nevertheless one can learn more than one is willing to admit.

I suppose the two people who had most influence on me as writers were Dietrich Bonhoeffer and Thomas Merton. In different ways they seemed to provide a pattern of contemporary sanctity to which I could respond and with which I could identify.

In July 1971 I was ordained priest at Ampleforth, a year earlier than usual since I had one more year of theology to do in Rome. This was because three of my contemporaries were being ordained at that time, having finished their four years of theology. For some years before ordination I had growing reservations about becoming a priest. It seemed to me that the connection between the monastic and priestly vocations was not altogether a happy one. After all, St Benedict had not been a priest and yet he was the spiritual father of the community. I wondered whether in some ways the two vocations did not pull in opposite directions: the monastic towards a simple, stable community life based on common prayer, a shared way of life and work and a certain amount of solitude and *fuga mundi*; the priestly vocation, especially according to the understanding found in the Second Vatican Council, tending rather towards an external apostolate, which meant leading a parochial community and being involved in a practical way in preaching the gospel and working among people. I felt the combination of the two states of life tended to identify the monastery with the clerical world rather than offering a pioneering and different way of life, open to the more radical and adventurous currents to be found in the Church and world of the time. In our case I wondered whether ordination did not provide a too easy and unthought-out justification for maintaining parishes, many of them far distant from the monastery, as well as giving the impression that the definitive step in a monk's life was ordination and not solemn vows.

On the other hand I realized that the issue was not a simple one. There is a deep and ancient tradition of missionary monasticism going back in British history to Celtic monks such as Columba and Aidan, the great missionary work of St Augustine and his companions, and the later achievements of Anglo-Saxon missionaries such as St Boniface. In addition one of the threads in English Benedictine history since the Reformation has been the missionary desire to convert England back to the ancient faith, a current that was particularly strong in the Ampleforth community. Indeed many of our parishes ante-dated the establishment of the community in England in the early nineteenth century after two centuries of exile on the Continent. The ideal of the priest-monk was deeply embedded and highly respected and had its own spirituality and aspirations. It was the obvious and cherished model at Ampleforth by which our monastic life was interpreted and lived, and provided one of the binding elements of our unity. So though some questions were beginning to be aired and the fact of non-priest monks in other communities was coming to be known, nevertheless it was largely taken for granted that, when the time came, one would be ordained priest.

So it was with rather ambiguous feelings that I faced the prospect of ordination myself. I think my main discernible motives were part loyalty and part conformity: to decline ordination in our context would have been highly 'singular', a course of action not recommended by St Benedict. It would have meant opting out of (and therefore appearing to criticize) much of the work undertaken by the community which involved the priesthood, especially parish work. But still it was not with any great expectations, and perhaps even with a slight sense of inner reluctance, that I came to the actual ceremony of ordination on 4 July 1971. But then something quite strange happened. As we were processing into the Abbey Church at the beginning of the Mass just in front of the Bishop, robed still as deacons, a very powerful sense came over me of the utter rightness of what I was about to do, of what was about to happen to me, to be ordained priest. I had never felt anything quite like it before: it was very strong yet gentle; it seemed to flow all around me like a tide of water or a strong light, not at all imaginary or subjective yet deeply interior and personal, as though bells were being sounded which a truer ear than my conscious intellectual mind could hear and respond to. It was somehow a gift of certainty that this ministry was what I was called to by God and that this moment was of great blessing and significance for the future. The meaning of sacrament came home to me very powerfully: an outward sign of inner grace, something given by God quite mysteriously, not merited or even thought of before. In many ways, indeed, it went against the grain of my intellectual convictions, which were somehow rendered in that moment not so much untrue as inopportune, like wearing jeans at a coronation. The moment was quite brief but it has stayed with me ever since and I have never had any doubts that I was meant to be a priest. Next day I celebrated my first Mass on my own with friends and relations. Afterwards I remember feeling a sort of helpless gratitude at the privilege of handling the mystery of the Body and Blood of Christ, of re-enacting his redeeming sacrifice for myself and others, of being a steward of God's mysteries, *alter Christus*. Ever since then I have treasured the opportunity to celebrate the Eucharist and the other sacraments, especially baptisms and weddings. I have learned too a lot from preaching: it has often been by trying to communicate something of the gospel that the truth it contains has come home to me for the first time. Also in the years that followed ordination I have often been happiest working on one of our parishes, at Liverpool, Leyland or at the local parish of Kirkbymoorside. It has given me an opportunity to work among and get to know ordinary working-class people, to share their problems and on occasion help them, as well as making many friends. I enjoyed the freedom of parish life and the chance of living with a small group rather than a large and more institutional community. I also grew to appreciate more the contribution of our parish fathers to the community, both past and present. The parishes had provided a good counterbalance to the more rarefied and separate world of Ampleforth and its school.

I returned to Ampleforth in the summer of 1972 after nearly eight years away studying. It was not an easy re-entry and I think the following few years were the most difficult and painful of my monastic life (so far!). A lot of it was my own fault: I found it well-nigh impossible to throw myself into the life of the community and the work of the school. I taught with reasonable competence and did discover to my surprise and delight a certain knack of getting on with adolescent boys, so that many friendships were formed. But at a deeper level there was an inner reluctance to commit myself. I found myself too often an observer and a critic rather than a participant. I felt that the whole place was grinding on in its accustomed grooves and not taking account of the new demands made on monastic communities for reform and renewal, and this disheartened me. I think I was better at talking about such renewal than living it in practice, but at the same time the problems were real ones which I felt could not indefinitely be swept under the carpet.

This situation led to a certain tension with Abbot Basil, who naturally wanted to see me take full part in the life of the place and take on in time positions of responsibility. He was disappointed and grieved, I think, when I wouldn't. It was of course very difficult for him, trying to steer a large community into new paths, and on occasion, perhaps, he let opportunities for decisive action pass, out of a deep reluctance to hurt people. Fortunately I do not think the real friendship between us was ever broken nor did he push me beyond the point where he thought I could go.

Another important element in this period was the work of the Monastic Theology Commission, which I found a great inspiration and support. Getting to know a group of people from other communities, working, laughing, discovering together, gave me a support for my own sanity. Living day to day at Ampleforth I often found that I was tempted to give up a dream and to doubt whether I had any grasp of the truth, and to think that They were right and we were wrong. I found the Monastic Theology Commission a focus and framework in which I could be more myself. It provided an opportunity to listen and to discuss on serious matters which very often was lacking at home. The sense of solidarity with a group and its working, the achievement of something worthwhile concerned with monastic life today, I found a great strengthening of faith in the basic value of a monastic life in the EBC.

This was the background to what was for me an abortive attempt to take part in a small experimental monastic venture at Little Crosby, near Liverpool. For a number of years ideas had been floating around the community of establishing some new offshoot of Ampleforth, either in the parish context or elsewhere. But these suggestions never seemed to get beyond the drawing-board stage. By the mid-1970s a group of us became determined to try to start something and put in a request to that effect in 1976 to Abbot Ambrose, who had been elected that year after Abbot Basil had become Archbishop of Westminster. In my own case the reasons were varied and mixed. Certainly dissatisfaction with my life in the Abbey played a part. Then there was the desire to test my urge to lead a simpler and more contemplative monastic life and start something new which would not be encumbered by the weight of history and existing commitments. These motives were sharpened by the departure of my closest friend in the community who decided to leave and get married. I felt somehow put on the spot by this as well as grieved: in many ways we felt the same and I thought I had to do something to get out of a rut.

The Abbot and council gave permission to three of us, somewhat reluctantly, I suspect, as the matter was very controversial in the community. After a certain amount of house-hunting we were lucky to be given a cottage on a Catholic estate just outside Liverpool and there we moved in October 1977. The intention was to be as self-sufficient as possible, lead a fairly strict life of prayer and study and take in guests who wanted to share the life for a longer or shorter time. I spent quite a lot of time, in addition to household chores, translating Rahner into English, while Father Thomas who was in charge worked at bookbinding in which he is a considerable expert.

For me, however, the venture did not turn out well. Valuable though it was, I found very soon that it was not for me; I needed a larger world, more freedom, intellectual stimulus and pastoral contacts. I could not live up to the image I had of myself as a simple contemplative monk. A dream had come true in the sense that flesh and blood had been given to a desire, yet I knew that I could not find in it the sort of perfect seal, the ideal for which I was searching. I found that traumatic. It cut away a good deal of confidence and made me feel very mistrustful of my own judgement: if I could be wrong about that I could be wrong about anything. Yet it did lead to a greater self-knowledge. It was another ring in the spiral of discovery that one's true self is a gift from God, not an achievement that one can plan. I had to accept myself because that was the self God made. I felt badly about leaving the other two to continue on their own, but after a couple of months I asked the Abbot to let me return. In fact I spent the rest of that year helping on our parishes, first at Liverpool and then at Leyland, while I continued with my Rahner translation. I enjoyed this and was in some ways reluctant to return to the Abbey, which however, I did in the autumn of 1978. Again re-entry was not easy, especially as one felt in oneself a sense of failure and a draining of self-confidence. But the brethren were remarkably understanding and gradually things have become easier.

Coming back to Ampleforth, I felt very strongly that my future, whether interior or exterior, was bound up with the future of the community. There was no way I could find a personal holiness or fulfilment except by living through the hopes and the fears, the pains and the blessings of a community. This had an effect on my prayer in that it gave me a greater sense of the value of petition, of storming heaven in order to change the future and to enable God to act. It was not that I had any clear idea what I was and am praying for, but rather that the truth should be seen, the will of God done. I was a part of that process, and often passivity – praying – was as important a part in that renewal as suggestions and advice.

This raises an important spiritual issue, the dialectic between trusting in God – waiting on his revelation and action – and responsible use of freedom, doing. There is no easy relation between these two. There is a time more for one, a time more for another, but both of them are needed. The danger of passivity on the one hand, or of 'programming' the Kingdom of God on the other, is very strong both in the individual and in a community, and I have not found a resolution of that tension. Perhaps it is a pattern which will be glimpsed only in eternity. One aspect of trusting in God is waiting and patient endurance. Yet individuals must not give up their dream, nor settle down into a sort of resignation of soul which abandons any deep hope of renewal of vitality, a renewal which can give new direction and vision to both the individual and the community.

This sort of suffering is particularly painful because it is found within the community, within a body of people who are dedicated to following Christ and living according to the Rule. Suffering which is undergone for the sake of the gospel, even though that can be painful, is somehow easier to bear because the case is clearer: it is easier to identify with the sufferings of Christ and therefore to hope in resurrection. But often suffering is living in a fog, not seeing clearly what the demands of the gospel are in our particular situation. Gradually I have come to see that in the will of God, which means accepting such a situation, there lies peace.

Somehow I feel now more able to contribute what I can in the community and leave the rest to God. The problems have not disappeared but the anxiety and worry have gone. In fact for the last year I have found myself teaching at Gilling Castle, the preparatory school near Ampleforth, owing to the untimely death of one of the brethren in April 1980. This has proved surprisingly satisfying, although I do not expect it to be a life sentence. Such is the Odyssey so far.

Some Reflections

1 *On prayer:* I think my commonest prayer has been the prayer of need: 'Lord, help me'. My greatest need has been for the increase and strengthening of faith and trust in the mysterious providence of God. Very often I have felt burdened by what seem insoluble problems springing either from my own weakness or from the state of things around me. But again and again a way out or a way through has unexpectedly appeared and faith and confidence in God have been strengthened. Gradually I have come to see that it is not our weakness but rather our seeming strength which is the greatest barrier to growth in faith, and therefore to the growth of freedom in the grace of God. It is the moments of helpless need which are the blessed times. It is striking that the key moments in the history of our salvation by God, the moments recorded in the Christian creeds, are moments of passivity not action: the 'Fiat' of our Lady to the Word becoming flesh, the crucifixion of Christ, his being raised from the dead. The whole of Christ's active ministry is passed over in order to highlight these cardinal points of powerlessness in which the creative Spirit of God is most powerfully at work. Mysteriously, too, these moments of powerlessness and of passion are moments of freedom: 'Let it be done unto me according to your word.' This has increasingly become for me the heart of prayer, a willingness to be carried wherever God wills, to stop trying to

programme the future or worry about the past, but simply to be led like a child.

2 *On suffering:* For me the chief form of suffering has been mental, not physical, as I have been blessed (so far) with good health. It is rather inner fear, feelings of guilt and failure, worry about the future for myself and others which have been most painful. What is most extraordinary is that gradually I have come to see that the most unwanted and painful inner suffering is actually a means of being drawn closer to God. The face of God as of one who loves and is lovable above all things is actually revealed through such experiences. The whole thing is most strange and paradoxical: what human lover would treat his beloved in this way? For me it is the most practical and genuine witness to the truth of the Christian mystery that personal suffering does bring greater peace of mind, a sense of joy and a greater capacity to love and be loved. At the time one can rage and try to escape, feel that one is going further and further away from God and that hope is really lost, and yet later one knows that only thus could one be given a deeper understanding and experience of the mystery of God. Through cross to resurrection is indeed the grammar of the language of the true God.

3 *On celibacy:* The single most difficult thing for me in being a monk has been celibacy. I have repeatedly thought of excellent reasons for not being celibate: of why I would be better off, happier, more fulfilled as a person, more creative, etc., if I were married and had a family. These reasons seem particularly convincing when things are difficult or I have just been with a happily married couple. And yet I am quite sure that God wants me to be celibate for his own mysterious purposes and that the path to genuine happiness for me lies there. Certainly there have been enough bits of evidence in my life, both positive and negative, to convince me of this: fidelity to being celibate has brought greater peace of mind, deeper prayer and warmer friendships, especially with women; while attempts to evade it have usually been disastrous, both emotionally and spiritually. As I have become more aware of my own weakness and inability to carry this particular cross on my own, so gradually it has become easier to entrust my own affections, emotions, bodiliness and sexuality to God and find there a gentleness and acceptance which is an assurance that I am indeed loved, body and soul, and that no part of me is either hidden or rejected but is, rather, enfolded in the

encompassing love and mercy of God. Out of that growing awareness come the freedom and the ability to love and be loved by others.

There is no doubt, however, that there is pain and suffering involved which it is important not to evade or disguise. For instance I have often felt extremely lonely because of being celibate and not having a relationship with another human being in which 'each is the other's best'. It has all seemed so pointless at times, an emotional cul-de-sac from which there is no way out. But gradually a light has begun to dawn in the heart of that darkness: 'Do not be afraid. You are not alone. I am with you until the end of days.' Somehow this begins to make sense of the pain though it is very difficult to work out a satisfactory intellectual rationale for it. It is certainly nothing to do with decrying sexual relationships or the value of marriage, still less with 'flight from woman'. I think that somehow for me it is a mysterious participation in the life-giving sacrifice of Christ, his passage to the Father. He entrusted everything to his Father, his body, his life, his future, his mission, his hope of immortality, his love of mankind. That was somehow his deepest service of his brethren. He died seemingly alone, a failure, abandoned. He had no human securities: he left it to his Father to work out his future. Yet he was not alone: he was guided through death to a new birth in the Spirit, and so appeared to his disciples, entrusting them with the charge to preach the gospel and promising to be with them always. Somehow for me celibacy is a sharing in Christ's passage to the Father and his service of the brethren. It is a stripping away of human supports but it is at the same time an emptiness which is gradually filled with the mysterious presence of God's Spirit which heals, enlivens and overflows to others as well as responding to them. This is often a hidden process, even from oneself, but there are moments and experiences which are a sign of its truth. A sort of test of its genuineness is that gradually God becomes more real and known and other people become closer. It is a lifelong affair whose true significance will only be revealed when God becomes 'all in all'.

Foreshadowings

DAME PAULA FAIRLIE

Sixteen years have passed since my reception into the Church. My vocation to the monastic life came simultaneously, although it took me four years to discover the true nature of the call. The complex pattern of my life resolved itself gradually and I can now see various strands which run through the whole and are slowly converging. I cannot follow them to the end, to the place of unity and completion, because my life goes on and I have not reached the vision of wholeness. But what I have seen, this I can try to describe.

I was born on 5 February 1940 in Uetersen, in Holstein, Germany. My mother, Olga Dluhosch, was of Austrian-Polish origin. She was born in 1906 at Karvin in Lower Silesia, then part of the Austrian Empire, now part of Czechoslovakia. She was a Catholic. Her family was among the many which had fled from Poland during the periodic uprisings, settling in Lower Silesia amid their fellow countrymen; some retained Polish as their mother tongue. I am told that we are descendants of a tutor to Jan Sobieski, one of the Polish kings. In 1907, when my mother was not yet a year old, her parents emigrated to Brazil with their two small daughters. Her father was an engineer, engaged on the construction of railway lines. The Dluhosch family lived as pioneers for a while before settling in Curitiba. A son was born, named Heinz.

These early years in Brazil had a powerful effect upon my mother and she regaled her own children with vivid tales of pioneer camps, colourful poisonous snakes, lethargic anacondas and dusky Amerindians. Just before the outbreak of the First World War the children were taken back to Europe on a liner by their mother, who left them there to receive their education while she returned to Brazil alone. The girls were cared for by an uncle and were in Austria during the war. In common with their fellow countrymen they endured hardship, which made my mother very frugal in later years.

My mother and her sister returned to Curitiba after the war. As Olga showed great promise as a violinist, one of her grandfathers offered to pay for her studies at the Conservatory in Vienna. Unfortunately the old man died before my mother could complete her training, and as he had made no financial provision for his granddaughter, Olga had to earn her own living in Europe. She trained as a secretary and her linguistic ability stood her in good stead. In her early twenties she moved to Hamburg, where she met my father.

My father, Wilhelm Feuerschütz, born in December 1909, was the eldest son of a well-established Holstein family. Our family tree can be traced back with a measure of accuracy for several hundred years. Originally belonging to the class of lesser nobility, they dropped the title in 1714. Holstein was once a Danish duchy and became part of the German Reich only in 1870, together with Schleswig. My family appears to have been one of the founding families of the small town of Uetersen and the family name appears in the earliest local records. One Feuerschütz with the biblical name of Zacharias seems to have been among the earliest Greenland whalers. Uetersen came into being in a flat marshland area, drained by dykes, with a harbour on a tributary of the river Elbe. As a duchy, Holstein felt the religious repercussions of the favoured Reformation policy of *cuius regio, eius religio* ('a country's ruler decides its religion'). There had been a religious foundation for women in Uetersen for many decades and the Lutheran church is still called *die Kloster Kirche*. As a child I never could understand who these mysterious 'Sisters' really were and I was rather nervous of passing their house.

The family business was trade in wood. Wood – hard woods which could be highly polished – came from Brazil, and soft woods from Scandinavia arrived at our little harbour. The smell of wood and playing among wood-shavings are part of our Feuerschütz childhood memories. Every generation played among the stacked wood in the lofts, visually stabbed by shafting sunbeams full of dancing dust. As a young man my father was sent as an apprentice to Sweden, in order to receive a sound basic knowledge of the trade. He too was an able linguist.

My parents met for the first time in Hamburg around the year 1930. My father was not yet twenty-one, my mother three years older. My mother was dark and vivacious, conscious of her ability to attract men, and a great talker. Wilhelm was a shy young man, of a steadier temperament, with a quiet sense of humour. I believe my mother had to make the first advances. They were very much in love and so weathered the family disapproval of a marriage with a 'foreigner' and a Catholic. My mother was only a nominal Catholic by this time but always clung to the name if not the belief. She could never live happily with the 'small-town mentality' of her in-laws, which was so different from her own cosmopolitan upbringing. My parents spent the first very happy years of their marriage in Brazil. I do not know why they returned to Hitler's Third Reich in the late 1930s. But it was only when they had settled in Uetersen that my brother was born and I arrived two years later.

The Second World War broke out a few months before my birth, and my father was called up. His father had been in the cavalry in the First World War but my father himself had no desire to fight. Since he was a married man with a young family he was treated with consideration. I believe he never used a weapon, although he had a pistol for self-defence, and served entirely in the capacity of interpreter when abroad. He was given compassionate leave at the time of my birth. My little brother joined him on the visit to the hospital after the delivery. When asked how his little sister Nora was, he replied, 'Little sister Nora says, "Quack quack"'. Apparently I was bawling my head off.

My father came on leave once again before he was taken prisoner in Africa with the remnant of Rommel's army, but I retain no conscious memory of this visit. So he was an unknown figure in my early childhood and largely remained so for much of my life. As I was born in wartime, I took sirens, bombings in nearby Hamburg, retreats into air-raid shelters and rationing for granted. During the worst time my brother and I slept fully clad in our nursery, boots on newspaper to save the bedclothes, rucksack and gas-mask beside us on a chair. We were fortunate to be in the British zone of occupation once Germany was defeated, and had quite a lot of contact with the 'Tommies', as my mother was acting as interpreter for a British officer. It also meant that we were treated warily by our countrymen. Sadly enough, the British officer fell in love with my mother and our home broke up.

St Thomas Aquinas declared that the grace of God does not destroy our human nature, but builds upon it and brings it to perfection. This is something which I came to accept whole-heartedly in later years, and, looking back at my early childhood, I also echo Wordsworth's belief that the child is father to the man.

The dominants of my early years are moments of wonder at natural beauty. I remember my passion for trees, especially a silver birch and willow growing in my grandparents' grounds. I remember the delight with which I saw a hedgehog, followed by a line of minute babies with soft white spines, moving among the stacked wood. I loved seeing dust dancing in sunbeams and the light shining on a huge chest of mixed grain which my grandmother scattered for her hens. Dew-bedecked spiders' webs wove their own enchantment, as did raindrops dripping off roof-edges.

Music was always there, the chamber music my mother played with her friends after we had been put to bed by the nursemaid. Then there were the Christmas Eve concerts in the Lutheran *Kloster Kirche*. But above all, there was the song of birds. Fairy stories were part of our daily life, as were the more mysterious tales of foreign lands. There were rides on the crossbar of my grandfather's bicycle into ripe cornfields taller than the child with him. The delight at the colour of poppies, at the deep blue cornflowers which twisted among the golden stalks, remains with me still. And the occasional pink sugar mouse was cause for rapture.

There was not much religious influence in my early years, although we lived in a predominantly Lutheran environment. My mother had retained vestiges of her Catholic belief and practice. So we always ate fish on Fridays. I think she sometimes went to Mass, but we never went with her. She retained a devotion to our Lady and as young children we wore miraculous medals round our necks. She may even have said some prayers with us at bedtime, but this I cannot recall.

Our Lutheran grandmother was the only devout Christian I knew. She was an upright woman, both physically and spiritually, and went regularly to church and her communion service. On Christmas Eve we children went with her and I think my mother played in the orchestra as it accompanied our lovely German carols. This was always a prelude to the festivities of *Heilig Abend*. On our return home there would be a solemn opening of the drawing room, when we children gasped at the pure white and silver beauty of the candle-bedecked Christmas tree. At Easter there was the symbol of the egg: the hidden life-potential of a fertile egg breaking out of the apparent tomb. The hatching of chicks made this clear, although I could not have verbalized it. We played a game of seeking the coloured eggs, surely symbolic of the search for the risen Lord, but at the time this was beyond our understanding.

In one of his letters C. S. Lewis told his friend Malcolm not to fear the apparent 'illusions' of memory. He was explaining that informed hindsight sometimes enables us to see the import of an event, the hidden glory within it, when the happening itself was not momentous. It is merely that we see it more clearly for what it is. This awareness of significance has come to me in later life.

I have frequently been perplexed when people express the desire to have 'religious experiences', or say that they have not had any. It seems to me now, in middle age, that any truly human event, however insignificant, is potentially a religious experience. Most reflective people seem to sense this. In the gospel we hear that Mary pondered in her heart and through this pondering in faith and love came to some measure of understanding of God's plan. She had to ponder, and so do we, if we seek meaning in our life. Perhaps most of us have some key experience which both unlocks the past and opens on to the future. This moment becomes the focal point of our personal integration. After that, all the apparently meaningless patches of light and darkness both before and after begin to form a whole. But still we see only in a mirror, darkly.

I have selected three memories from my early childhood in Germany, not only because they are clear but also because they became significant foreshadowings of later spiritual realities. God comes to us as we are, in the way in which we can apprehend him, and to me he has always come in the swiftly passing moments of ordinary life. The moment I have become aware, in that moment he has gone. So there have been only flashes of light, both in intellectual apprehension and in the darkness of faith. These moments have always brought me great peace. But I have had no vision and my way is always the dark way of faith.

How can one describe the dawning of consciousness? It seems to me that I was long asleep in darkness when the darkness was dispelled by light, white light, and I both saw and experienced. I was only a baby, scarcely able to clutch the bars of my play-pen. A moment before, I had felt myself swung through the air and placed on my feet. I looked up at my mother and cried. Dark enfolded me again but my baby mind held its first memory. It was a memory of movement from darkness into light and back into darkness again.

The next memory which stands out is of sitting on a hillock near home on a summer's afternoon. My brother was playing in the hedgerows while I sat on the grass, looking at golden coltsfoot. I was sitting and thinking about a fairy story we had been told and was vaguely conscious of the bleating of tethered goats and the tinkling of their bells. I cannot have been more than four years old. After a while the movement of the clouds attracted my attention and I gazed up. A towering cumulus cloud moved swiftly towards me. I looked and was awed. A strange sense of dread and otherness came upon me. I was so small and the cloud so great. In real fear I quickly ran home. I had become aware of the numinous and of my own insignificance.

It must have been early autumn, one of those chill days before the leaves have really coloured. I was walking to school, so it must have been some time in 1946, and I was wearing a blue coat made from material my father had sent from Africa. The war had ended and a few prisoners of war were returning home. My mother had already decided to marry her British officer, so we moved house. I was thoughtful as I made my way along the cobbled street and avoided looking at the casual passers-by. I had been warned never to talk to strangers. I became aware of the tall figure of a man coming towards me, looking at me intently. I gazed back, despite the warning, and thought that perhaps he was distantly familiar. We kept looking at each other until we drew level. Then he bent down and asked: 'Are you Nora Feuerschütz?' Surprised, I replied: 'Yes.' He said: 'I am your father.' This is the first memory of him which I have, but from that day I was fascinated by eyes and by their power of communication. Words do not penetrate so deeply into the human heart as a loving glance.

The movement from darkness to light and back into darkness is the common rhythm of natural life and it is also a spiritual rhythm. God is a hidden God, both knowable and supremely unknowable. Moments of intellectual awareness are movements into the light, moments of intuitive awareness are movements into the dark. Often, long stretches of our life are seen as times of shadow, although subsequent examination shows that there were periods bathed in the glory of light. The next part of my life, for many years, seemed to me covered by the darkness of fear and negation. I now see this time of dread more truly as a time of preparation and hidden growth, and the joy hidden in it becomes ever stronger.

My mother's second marriage in 1946 was a disaster almost from the beginning and eventually ended in divorce thirteen years later. But despite the obvious unhappiness for all concerned, these years were not wasted.

For me there were great changes. I lost the companionship of my brother and this was a deep hurt. I had to cope with loneliness and solitude, which increased when we set sail for the Port of London in a small packet steamer in January 1948. I left behind the whole of my former world, all the warmth of affection lavished upon me by my numerous relations, my language, my childhood.

The voyage took longer than anticipated because of the rough seas. Yet even on board I found kindness. I was fascinated by the size of British coinage and had a small collection of old pennies. These I showed to anyone interested and was quite disconcerted when a kindly soldier gave me a small silver sixpence in return for six large pennies. Perhaps that was symbolic too.

London was wreathed in thick yellow fog. The train journey to Shifnal was dismal. It all echoed how I felt. I had never seen tenement houses before and I found the industrial Midlands dreary and confining beyond belief. People were kind to the strange German child but it was a while before a semblance of happiness returned. I suffered from dreadful nightmares, which lasted several years, and then I had stomach trouble.

Our move to Surrey, into those kindly wooded hills, the winding country lanes and beautiful old houses, helped me. I enjoyed attending the junior school in Byfleet and made my first English friend. Pamela was the first of many friends throughout the years, but she marks a turning-point in my life. I had always been a tomboy and rather wild, and now these energies were channelled into imaginative play. I read avidly and soon became familiar with all things English like nursery rhymes and English children's classics; and I identified quickly with my companions. But the horrid fact remained: I was German, and Germans were understandably unpopular. It was rare for a child to taunt me with this, but when I was taunted, I was a spitfire. I had barely mastered sufficient English to say, 'You are unfair. I am a child and I did not make the war', but I did say it. And I wept bitterly. It took me many years to become reconciled to my nationality and even now I am still vaguely apprehensive that people will like me the less for it.

I attended the Byfleet junior school for about a year before we moved to Worcester Park, Surrey. There the school in Malden Manor was larger and there was not the same feeling of friendliness as in Byfleet. I received my secondary school education at Wimbledon County Grammar School, where I was from 1951 to 1958. The teaching throughout my period of Engish schooling was excellent and I was fortunate in having dedicated and understanding teachers. It was probably this as much as anything else which made me desire to make teaching my profession.

Nothing particularly significant spiritually happened to me in these years. Through my teachers and the undenominational religious instruction we received, I learnt something about Christianity. But it made no appeal. I was aware of God and joined in the daily school assemblies, but I was happiest outside amid grass and trees. Assemblies for worship seemed so unreal and did not have any conscious effect upon my daily life. The person of Christ, presented visually and orally in the 'meek and mild' tradition, was the greatest stumbling-block. I wanted strong personalities who could convince me, and, much as I admired the Church of England teachers, I could not understand their religious beliefs. So I was both attracted and repelled.

I was sent to Sunday School for a while. I detested the classes and considered churchgoing a social gathering for most adults. The conversation after church seemed so trivial. I wanted something that mattered all the time, which really penetrated one's being. I spent many Sundays and holidays riding my bicycle along quiet Surrey lanes. I used to stop at churches and gaze at the encircling graveyards. The silence and peace appealed to me, although the church interior was often so incredibly empty. It was a shell, with no light anywhere.

My strong natural love of beauty made me responsive to poetry. Even poems like 'Silver' and 'Home Thoughts from Abroad' spoke to me of a hidden reality, a mysterious realm of the spirit which nature both revealed and hid. So I was aware that there was more to life than material existence, although what it was eluded me. I responded also to Greek dancing, which is largely interpretative, and found I could express more in movement than in words. Painting was also a joy, although I was never more than mediocre. But I loved colour, especially the warm colours of autumn, which symbolized even then the maturity for which I yearned. I remember so clearly looking out of my bedroom window in Worcester Park, watching the rain trickle round hard green apples on the boughs of the tree nearest the house. I identified with the hard green apples and tried to write a poem. Only one line remains, and it makes me smile:

> Small green apples feel the tears of heaven.

As I look back, this period of thirteen years seems as pale and colourless as the adolescent girl I then was. I felt intensely and could express little. I only felt fully alive in a thunderstorm, which both exhilarated and frightened me.

There was friendship, especially with a junior school friend called Michael, who lived in the same avenue. There were schoolmistresses who took a personal interest in me; one of them is still a friend after almost thirty years. Another opened to me the wonder of Wordsworth's poetry, especially parts of the 'Prelude' and 'Tintern Abbey', and I lived vicariously in them. I was an omnivorous reader and enjoyed trying to read the *Confessions* of St Augustine at the age of twelve. Later I was interested in Plato's imagery of the cave and the shadows on the wall. All this spoke to me far more than Christianity and I termed myself a Deist.

At grammar school my aggressive streak came out during Religious Instruction classes. I was quite ready to argue with anyone and am amazed that the long-suffering deputy headmistress in fact encouraged me to do so. I demolished Christianity to the best of my ability in discussion after discussion. I loathed piety and the veneers of religiosity which people seemed to put on. But it was the miracles which I remember best. I felt convinced that they had no supernatural origin: it was merely the power of suggestion bringing out the best in people. I rationalized everything and could not understand how people could be so gullible. Yet in my heart I envied them. I remained outwardly scornful, even while searching in secret.

At the age when some of my contemporaries began reading the Bible assiduously, underlining favourite verses, I turned to Methodism for some five weeks. The Methodists seemed so wholesome and friendly, and a basic simplicity in their services appealed to me. I realized too that if ever I did become a Christian, it would have to be a total commitment. I was not ready for that. At this stage I knew nothing of nuns, except that one of my temporary teachers had entered an Anglican order. I saw her in full attire one day when I was waiting at the bus stop. She looked at peace. Many months later I saw her again, in secular clothes. She looked wretched. I was too young to say anything, but I have never forgotten her.

My greatest personal loss in these years was the death of my Lutheran grandmother in January 1953. I had seen her a few weeks before, when she lay pale and gaunt in her bed, dying of cancer. She loved singing and asked me to sing for her. I sang to her in English and since it was Christmas time I remember choosing 'Away in a manger' as one carol. I was there amid her children and eldest grandchildren when she received the last rites of her Church. She tried to comfort us with her strong faith. Her death was a severe blow to us all. I was told later that she had never really worried about what would happen to me, saying 'Nora knows her own mind'. This seemed to be enough for her.

In the autumn of 1958 I began my two-year course of teacher training at Gipsy Hill Training College, then on Kingston Hill. I qualified before my twenty-first birthday and spent three years teaching at Hersham, Surrey. The years from 1958 to 1963 were not momentous spiritually, either.

The most powerful influence was the then Principal of the College, Frances Batstone. She had a brilliantly logical mind and was a convinced Christian. I used to attend some services led by her in our Nissen hut chapel and one day almost gasped with unbelief when she said that she believed in angels. I had never gone beyond the visual imagery and this pulled me up short. I began to consider Christianity a little more seriously.

Since I had never been confirmed, it was suggested by our divinity lecturer that it might be as well if I received some instruction. She herself was an Anglo-Catholic and introduced me to St Stephen's, Gloucester Road. I was not sure what to do. I had an acute prejudice against the Roman Catholic Church at the time, the result of years of unconscious indoctrination, but none the less was also attracted towards it. In fact, my first Catholic friend Mary had once taken me to Mass in the Brenninkmeyer Library on Kingston Hill. But I accepted the Church of England instruction for six months. At the end of it I was not convinced and did not want to be confirmed. When I told the Vicar this, he advised me to make a leap into the dark. I made it and remained in the dark. The one positively good outcome was my introduction to another Anglican clergyman a couple of years later, who was skilled in counselling. He helped me to go on searching and on his advice I applied to Bedford College, University of London, to read History Honours.

For the three years before this, I lived in a bed-sitter in Surbiton, close to my Catholic friend. I attended the local Anglican church, observed church discipline and spent some time in meditation. But I did not believe. I had several boy-friends, but none of their minds attracted me and so the friendships were all short-term. Unhappily, a married man fell in love with me and this added complications, as I found him attractive. It was hard to act on Christian principles and I was desperately unhappy for a while. At this time I painted a picture of a young woman – in fact, two young women – on a ledge down a crevasse. One was looking down into the abyss, the other was reaching upwards towards the sun and grassy plains above her head. This was how I felt: I was quite undecided whether my death urge was stronger or my life urge.

From 1963 to 1966 I was at Bedford College, London. These years were vitally important for me and at the beginning of my final year I was received into the Catholic Church. The story may be of interest as an account of how God slowly brought divergent strands of my life into unity and how a thoroughly disintegrated personality like my own could come to a measure of wholeness. For me it was the greatest blessing of my life.

One branch of history which I was reading was called political theory and it was literally that. But political theory is based on philosophy. In my reading I had to study Plato, Augustine,

Aquinas and many other writers. I had to read much relating to Christianity and the contact with the most brilliant minds of the West made me realize that belief was not so stupid. I was aware that these powerful minds, so much better than my own, did believe in the supernatural; and many were convinced Christians, and Catholics at that. The more I read, the more I became convinced that faith and reason were not intrinsically in opposition. I could not yet appreciate St Anselm's dictum: 'I believe in order to understand', but I realized that faith alone could provide a key to what was otherwise a meaningless jumble. I had two Catholic lecturers, both converts, and their unspoken testimony was also a sign. I read on and became convinced that if there was a God who had revealed himself, who had 'redeemed the world' (whatever that meant), then the Catholic belief was the logical outcome. But I did not have the gift of faith.

Several of my closest friends were Catholics, although one was lapsed. I used to go with her to Mass because she had the duty to go and it did not matter to me where I went. So I was a regular Mass-goer at the time of the Second Vatican Council and saw the changes from Latin into the vernacular.

From my teens onwards people tended to confide in me and often I attempted to shoulder burdens which were beyond my strength. This happened too in my early twenties and the problems of a married friend drained me emotionally and physically. I got so tired that I was tempted to take my life. My hand was stayed, but the emotional revulsion, the shame and contempt I felt for myself, seemed to force me down into the abyss. When I could bear no more, I discovered a deep life-urge in me which made me want to climb out. This was in 1965, just before I was due to go on holiday to Florence. I had changed my special subject, finding medieval monasticism too dull, and had opted for Renaissance Studies. This meant that I had to learn Italian, as most of my texts were in that language. A fellow student recommended a convent in Florence, where the guest-mistress was German-born. Thus there would be less language difficulty. I was glad to leave England for a while. I needed to make a new start. I took a plane to Pisa on 3 July 1965. In London it was raining.

I arrived in Florence in the darkness of an early July morning. I had travelled throughout the night and was exhausted physically and mentally. It was a good tiredness, making the past recede and the present less anxious. So it was with a certain sense of expectancy that I stood in Florence in the darkness which heralded the dawn. Gradually the sky turned white and then the radiance of a new day dawned upon the dark encircling hills.

So far my search for beauty and truth had been only partially satisfied by nature, art and literature. The human element had been missing and thus even the pagan awareness of human dignity did not penetrate my consciousness. I had never awoken into life through human love.

I cannot now recapture the wonder of that awakening. The vibrant colour of brilliant geraniums, the shimmering groves of silvery olive trees, the stark contrast of dark upward-thrusting cypresses, the rich brown earth of Tuscany, all spoke to my senses. But they were only the outer symbols of an inner thrust into life. I have never lived as intensely as I did in that month of July. My gift for sheer enjoyment welled up into laughter and I became exuberantly alive.

It came about through my friendship with Madre Geltrude. She had subjected me to a quizzical appraisal and then her deceptively sleepy-looking blue eyes had smiled. There had been an unspoken bond: we were both of German origin, although naturalized citizens of our adopted countries, and deep inside us we were always aliens. Neither of us was in any way sophisticated and both had artistic bents without being artists. So despite an age difference of almost twenty years, we were immediately in harmony. This meant that I was able to ask her about what still puzzled me in Christian belief. I know one question was, 'Why did there have to be an incarnation?' I do not remember her answer, but it satisfied me.

We went for walks in the Tuscan fields, and visited a village called La Petraia. There we sat watching dragonflies skimming over a pond at evening time. The trees were reflected in the water and I was conscious again of thinking that probably I preferred the mystery of reflections to the clearness of reality. This had always puzzled me since Plato maintained that our world was but the reflection of reality and I seemed to prefer unreality, and surely that was wrong? But somehow that did not seem to matter: it was good to be alive.

All the while I attended daily Mass and prayed for the gift of faith. But I seemed no nearer belief, despite my intellectual acceptance of Christianity. Then one day Madre Geltrude and I knelt alone in church. She quietly turned to me and, pointing to the tabernacle, asked: 'Ist Er da?' ('Is he there?'). Did I believe in the Real Presence of Christ? Poised between the answers 'No' and 'Yes', neither of which I wanted to give, I suddenly heard myself saying 'Yes'. In that moment I received the gift of faith, which has ever remained with me.

The next memory had been foreshadowed by my cloud experience as a small child. Deep within the human psyche volcanic mountains and dense cloud have always formed the visual imagery of revelations of God, theophanies, so it is hardly surprising that my own minor 'awarenesses' have taken place on hillsides or gentle slopes.

After I had received the gift of faith I was silently inebriated for many days. On one of these days I made a trip to San Cresci in the Mugello. There among the terraced slopes and deserted farm-houses Madre Geltrude and I walked and talked, often laughing for sheer joy. I was very happy. Towards evening we sat down on a small hill. Cattle were moving slowly in the deep valley and birds were swooping low beneath us. We now sat in silence, the sun still pleasantly warm on our backs. I became powerfully aware of God's presence. It was absolutely overwhelming. I had to close my eyes and could hardly breathe; his presence was almost tangible. He was all around me, enfolding me in the warm evening air.

This experience has never been repeated, but the happiness of it comes back whenever I feel the sun warm on my back. Sometimes when I am gardening this gladness comes upon me. I understand the value of memory and appreciate the psalms in which the Israelites recalled God's saving help. The remembrance gives one confidence in the present moment and allows one to hope in the future. Simple awareness has sometimes come to me when I have heard people talking about God or something beautiful. I would feel my heart glowing within me for the moment, in affirmation of the recognized truth. Perhaps this is how the disciples on the road to Emmaus responded to the sensed but unrecognized presence of the Lord. These are all small and simple touches, but full of reassurance. The uncanny troubles me and like an animal with raised fur I feel shivers down my spine until the moment is passed. I think we probably all react like that, so it scarcely bears mentioning.

On my return to England I began receiving instruction in the Catholic faith, although this proved a formality rather than a basic need, and I was received into the Church on Saturday, 2 October 1965. My instructor was Fr John Davies, OFM Cap., then in Erith, Kent. On the next day I went to Southwark Cathedral and was confirmed, taking the name Paula. This was a moment of personal dedication and I asked God to show me what he wanted. I was convinced that I had a call to the religious life.

All this happened in the autumn and autumn has always been my season. In childhood I loved the warmth of colour and the maturity of fruitfulness, longing to be grown-up. In my religious life autumn has been the season for all decisive steps, including clothing and solemn profession. The Feast of All Saints has come to symbolize the spiritual in-gathering of my own life, linking me with the 'cloud of witnesses' who have influenced my development.

In October 1965, knowing that for me Christianity had to be all or nothing, I mentally prepared myself for the religious life. I wanted all, and nothing else would do. The months of my final year at Bedford College were a time of light, a time of sudden intellectual illumination. I was perplexed by the mystery of the Communion of Saints, by our relationship with God and with our fellow men. How were these things related, how could one love both God and man? I was walking back to College after early morning Mass when I mentally saw a hill. The summit represented God. A whole crowd of people, well spread out, were beginning to climb up the hill. The further up they went, the closer they came to God and each other. That was the answer. Some five years later I was delighted to discover that Dorotheus of Gaza had taught his hearers with a similar image, that of a circle with radiating spokes, the centre of which was God. It has always been a joy to me when my own 'discoveries' have proved to be entirely orthodox, already propounded many centuries ago. The human intellect has not changed much since the beginning of recorded time.

Only a few months of my life as a Catholic have been spent in secular environments. I do not regret this. My only Easter as a lay person I spent in Florence, devoting the vacation ostensibly to preparing for Finals, and actually to sheer enjoyment of life. Probably this was a period akin to the state of being in love, when one's senses are sharpened and the commonplace becomes full of glory. The climax came for me during the Easter Vigil. A few of us had gone into the hills to a small parish church for the celebration and joined the local peasants at their worship. There was an overwhelming sense of joy: everyone looked radiant. The lighted candle, the flowers and coloured eggs, the happy faces, the enthusiastic singing were intensely moving. I walked back to the convent in a quiet daze of satiety. A light rain was falling. Raindrops were shimmering on the olive trees that radiant night. There was a thunderstorm next day, followed by bright sunshine. I went alone into the garden, intoxicated by the scent of wet earth, by the rapture of lilac blossom and by the radiant colour of the tulips. It was almost more than I could bear, wild beyond the senses, and I went into the longing ecstasy which music occasionally arouses. The heavens could be opened: I could finally see . . . and then came the dropping back to earth. I was in a spring garden, the sun was shining from a stormy sky.

The theme of light and darkness in my life, which was foreshadowed by my first memory, has been a constant rhythm. At first I regarded darkness as a menacing chaos which threatened to disintegrate me. The horror of a storm at sea when I first crossed the Channel left me with an especial dread of that devouring Mother. But I have now come to see darkness as that primeval chaos over which the Spirit of God hovers, re-creating me, bringing me to another birth. We have so many small deaths to die. I value my time in darkness, my not knowing, even my pain, as I then simply have to abandon myself to God. So my prayer becomes a little more humble; I stop trying to organize my own life and I rest in him. Often this self-abandonment comes only when I have inwardly shed my tears of anger and limitation and have accepted again that God is greater than I.

During the Easter holiday I asked the Mother General of the Sisters of Montalve whether I could join her community when I had taken my Finals. I was accepted and left England – I thought for ever – on 24 June 1966. The next four years were a real testing. I went through a lengthy probation, was clothed in October 1967 and made my simple profession in October 1969. By then it was clear to me that a life of teaching combined with an attempt at religious life in community was not possible for me. It had to be all or nothing. The aftermath of the Second Vatican Council seemed to show that there was no future for the so-called active orders in areas of education and social work. Either one had to be a dedicated lay person or enter an enclosed community. Twelve years later I have come to doubt this assumption. The present-day trend seems to be towards active involvement by everyone, even enclosed Religious. This does leave me wondering what will happen to those of us who have a vocation to a simple monastic life and not to the market place. But at the time I thought a transfer to a Benedictine community in England would provide the answer.

These years in Italy were not happy ones. I had too many rigid preconceptions and one of them was that friendship between Religious of the same community was not acceptable. This meant that I had unwittingly opted for emotional impoverishment and this retarded my development. I had bypassed the human too often and this impoverished me spiritually. It was only some years after I began my religious life that I realized I had been bypassing the Person of Christ and so missing the point of Christianity altogether. As far as spirituality was concerned, I could have belonged to Old Testament times, although I was using Christian terminology. I seemed to understand the Way of the Cross, the agony of Gethsemane, and identified with them, but I could not get through to the glory of the resurrection or the Person of the risen Lord. That was the key experience that lay ahead, which my meeting with my father had foreshadowed.

The undertaking of celibacy had not unduly bothered me when I entered the religious life. Gradually I came to understand that it is not the absence of the physical which hurts most, but the renunciation of deep personal commitment to a human other. On the day of my clothing in Italy, when the bridal theme was dominant, I felt a sudden upsurge of bitterness. I had freely accepted permanent sterility. I would always be barren. It took me long years to work through, to accept the fruitfulness of spirit which God offered me. At a time when the going was hard, I wrote the following, invoking an imaginary companion:

> Dark silhouette in simple beauty
> outlined truth against the sky.
> Evening stillness.
> We gaze where a startled bird chatters unseen.
> We gaze together.
> The answer lies not in the flesh,
> the search is not for sensuous rapture –
> It goes beyond to Him who is.
> The answer lies not in the flesh,
> not in desire yielding to unity,
> symbolic quest for wholeness given and received.
> The answer lies not in ourselves.
> Dark silhouettes against the sky.
> Sky of desert, sky of sea.
> Dark wisps of cloud hair,
> deep pools of quiet eyes,
> quiet eyes which gaze and cannot fathom.
> Quiet eyes which see and do not see.
> Cool hands linked in flowing harmony.
> Dim awareness of Presence experienced as absence,
> spurred on by fulfilment in utter unfulfilment,
> we walk together in the darkening night.

It was a bright April day in 1970 when I arrived at Stanbrook Abbey. I was still somewhat numb after parting with my Italian

Sisters and apprehensive about the future. Did I have a vocation to the Benedictine way of life? Once again I had left the known to begin in the totally unknown, trusting that God was with me.

The welcome I received dispelled my doubts. The ceremony of receiving a new entrant made a deep impression on me and became symbolic. I knocked at the huge enclosure door which divided the secular from the monastic world and was drawn in. I followed a group of nuns to the church. They were singing Psalm 121: 'I rejoiced when I heard them say, "Let us go to God's house".' After a short period of prayer, the nuns processed out and drew up in a double line down the long cloister, with the Abbess at the very end. I had to pass through this anonymous group of almost seventy nuns to reach the Abbess for the traditional kiss of peace. It was a nerve-racking experience to walk on, seemingly alone, but I kept my eyes on the goal and got to safety! It helped me in later months to remember this and just to go on when the going was hard.

I was still very impressionable at the age of thirty and very responsive. But the move to a totally different environment also made it clear to me how immature I still was and how basically insecure. So it was a time of turmoil as I had to be reformed inwardly and outwardly. I was fascinated by the paradox of the seed dying into life, a text which occurred in the Office for 23 April, only a day after my entrance. This was what had to happen to me and I did not like the dying process. I experienced myself as an unresolved person and it was explained to me that there was such a thing as creative disintegration. We appear to be in a state of chaos, but this chaos is akin to the primeval chaos over which the Spirit of God constantly hovers, calling us to life. It was fine as theory, but I clung tenaciously to the line of the Benedictine Rule which says: 'With a silent mind hold fast to patience.' I used a similar image later, when it was my turn to support newcomers, but thought more in terms of a caterpillar undergoing transformation as a chrysalis, before emerging as a butterfly. I think the chrysalis stage needs much sympathetic understanding. Outwardly nothing is happening; there is just a hard casing, no sign of progress. Inwardly much is happening and there is transformation. But the onlooker needs real faith and patience, the readiness to wait until the growth is complete. It cannot be hurried. Sometimes there is not this understanding, so the final emergence of the butterfly is delayed.

I gradually came alive again at Stanbrook. My dormant sense of humour began to express itself in the occasional cartoon and I rejoiced in the balance of the life and sense of normality. I was not yet a gardener, but my happiest day was the one on which about twenty nuns were engaged upon potato-lifting. It was a warm sunny day and some Sisters wore large straw hats on top of their veils, and the strange variety of working clothes rejoiced my heart. I liked the tiredness at the end of the day and felt that I was now finally doing what I had always wanted to do. I was close to the soil, to basic being.

It was in the early months that I was given the key experience which made sense of my life and search for God. Personal relationships had always been my weak point, although I was a friendly child. I had never felt secure once my home broke up, and since my mother found me difficult to deal with, I came to consider myself basically unlovable. So I became an onlooker on life and acute diffidence expressed itself in an aggressive manner of speech. This I had to work at very hard and was once given the task of reading through the Rule and writing down how a monk ought to speak: 'quietly, gently and humbly' at all times and in all circumstances. Furthermore I did not like myself, despite the fact that many people throughout the years had become and remained friends. So there was a lack of basic acceptance and without this one is building on sand. Everyone around me seemed so self-reliant and basically happy, and I envied them. I developed an identity crisis. I did not seem to know who I was and when advised to be simply 'myself', I was in despair.

However, in the glorious days of late October I was in retreat before my clothing as a Benedictine novice. The conferences were the best I had ever had, adapted to my needs and satisfying. One must have been on God's love for me. I had always found this difficult to understand and since the Person of Christ had never really become alive for me in a deep personal way, I could not grasp how God's love manifests itself to us through other human beings. In this frame of mind I encountered the Abbess in the cloister. She smiled at me in passing and as our eyes met I suddenly understood. At least, I had the germ of understanding, although it will take the whole of my life to understand fully. I rushed off to my cell and started painting what I had recognized. The end product was pretty hopeless but afforded me great satisfaction.

The picture consisted of four images: dark eyes representing God's creative love; an embryo representing a person being called into being through love (I printed Psalm 138 underneath it for clarification). Then there was a picture of a person immersed in water, to which I added fish in case that wasn't obvious and wrote 'O purify me, Lord' beside the caption 'Purifying'. That represented what love does to us: it purifies and cleanses us. The final image caused me more trouble. It had to represent self-giving love; eventually I thought a chalice and open hands reaching towards it might convey the idea. It bore the caption 'A grain of wheat must die'. On the back of the picture I wrote explanatory notes: 'Identity crisis being resolved: hidden growth in dark. What has grown needs to be cleansed: result of human frailty, etc. Love which gives itself despite – because of – our unworthiness. Which evokes our active response.'

At last I had recognized that love was the answer and that only love itself can create the outwardgoing response in the other. Love cannot exist in a void and has to diffuse itself. It is dynamic and active, ever flowing, ever free. This I only understood much later, when I had a self with which to respond. But the answer had been given. It is the personal love of God which calls us into being, makes us capable of loving him and his creatures. We can only become ourselves in response to love first given to the loveless. Finally I began to understand what St John meant when he wrote, 'God's love for us was revealed when he sent his only Son into the world. This is the love I mean, his love for us, not ours for him . . . Since God has loved us so much, we also should love one another.'

Subsequent human failure and weakness have never dimmed that moment of grace. That moment of recognition, foreshadowed by my encounter with my father so many years before, finally made me a Christian. I now knew that Christ is the only way to the Father and that I had to come to him. We become what we love and I loved what I had seen. With the passing of the years I am ever more aware how much we need human example in our search, at least in the beginning. We need to see in human flesh the transformation of the merely natural into the fully human. So I have come to rejoice in St Irenaeus's saying, 'The glory of God is man fully alive'. The key had been given, even though it was not for the door to life in Stanbrook.

Despite my real happiness in the monastic life, I still had problems. The 'creative disintegration' I was experiencing made me tense, so it was hardly surprising that I was deemed unfit for life in community. I very much wanted to be accepted, so some of my behaviour was classed as 'seeking affection', when more truly it was seeking support. This caused me acute anguish. Combined with self-pity and the knowledge that my emotional development was way behind my intellectual ability, it made me feel increasingly that I was in the 'lame dog' category. Naturally my self-centredness was obvious to my novice mistress, whom I can now appreciate wholeheartedly since I am in a similar job, and she did her utmost to help me emotionally and prepare me for conventual life. In the end I was not accepted for simple profession. The reason given was my lack of 'affective maturity'. This quotation from *Perfectae Caritatis* (the Second Vatican Council's Decree on the Renewal of Religious Life) has since made me smile rather wryly. God had revealed his perfect love for me, but it had not borne any apparent fruit.

I left on 1 September 1972.

> My son, if you desire to serve the Lord,
> prepare yourself for an ordeal.
> Be sincere of heart, be steadfast,
> and do not take fright when disaster comes.
> Cling to him, and do not leave him . . .
>
> (Sir. 2.1–3)

With these verses from the Book of Ecclesiasticus well in mind, I began my third novitiate since 1966 at Talacre Abbey, North Wales. On 31 October 1972 I was again clothed as a Benedictine novice. Despite a sense of acute failure, I had to go on. And this seemed to be what God wanted.

The month I spent in secular life before coming to Wales was a month of blessing. My one prayer was 'What does God want?' I had sincerely tried to become what seemed required of me at Stanbrook and had failed. I could not have tried harder. That was the point. Now I had to entrust myself to God in complete darkness and really be one of the poor who has no one except God. I am grateful beyond words for this experience. I had nothing to hope for and so the smallest joy was my daily bread, received from the hand of a loving Father. The idea of 'the poor of Yahweh' had appealed to me greatly: those underprivileged of the Old Testament who through their deprivation and power-lessness found a way to be open to God. Their prayer echoes through the psalms and their utter confidence in God when everything seemed to gainsay it had always moved me. Now I was able to touch the fringe of that experience.

The other blessing was the awareness of having been loved, and the loving support of my former Abbess and novice mistress, who seemed to share my suffering, strengthened me. I eventually thought that my 'ejection' by Stanbrook was another birth and this time the umbilical cord was cut. I was now myself, a separate being, capable of forming personal relationships. So the identity crisis was over. God had given me myself.

The community at Talacre had been severely tried that year. Six nuns had died, including the Abbess, Dame Flavia Garland, so there was not much to attract me when I came to Wales. But I was convinced that I had a monastic vocation. It did not matter what happened to me because God would not abandon me. Here was a challenge and I was still young enough to take it on. I was also impressed by the cheerful courage the nuns seemed to have, so I asked to join them.

I was determined that at least the outward signs of a losing battle should disappear. So I tackled the overgrown area around the house for the next few years, spending every spare moment in a battle against brambles and nettles. This helped me psychologically and I rejoiced at every sign of new life when clumps of grass were lifted to disclose bulbs bravely bursting forth into the light. Every marigold grown from a seed was a miracle and at last there was a semblance of what the garden might have been once and could be again. Now much of my work is maintenance, but the battle goes on. If the garden were to become a wilderness again, for me it would symbolize the end.

Inside the house I was able to help sort out and clean up where others lacked the time to do so. The gardening helped to empty my mind and brought me a measure of peace. The housework helped some others to live in a less cluttered environment and a few of us benefited from a semblance of more gracious living. I have always needed a clean and spacious environment: the lack of one fills me with the horror of claustrophobia, from which I suffered for a while at Talacre. Part of my nature as a woman demands a home to care for and the attempt to create a pleasanter place to live in fulfils this. Unfortunately not everyone feels the same.

Having worked away at my environment, I found that I was being rooted without realizing it. All the while I was given much affection and understanding and came to realize how suffering we all are. This made me more compassionate and more determined than ever to fulfil Ruysbroeck's exhortation: 'Be kind, be kind, and you will be saints.' Probably consistent kindness is the hardest of all disciplines.

The foundations of my monastic life were laid at Stanbrook. They are good foundations and I am increasingly grateful for the excellent intellectual and spiritual formation I received. Perhaps I have become somewhat anti-intellectual at times, when life as experienced and life in theory seem to lack cohesion. I naturally tend to think in pictures, imagery, and am not capable of abstract thought. I want ideas rooted in the ground of my being, part of me as I am, and not something 'way out there' which means nothing in the life I lead. I was once told that the monastic life itself would teach me and it has, quite quietly and naturally through my endeavour to live faithfully according to the Rule I have freely accepted. So although my life has been very enclosed and circumscribed in many ways these last nine years, I have grown.

There has not been much intellectual stimulus, so I have depended almost entirely upon the Scripture readings of the various Offices, and on my odd moments of prayerful reading, for spiritual nourishment. However, I have been able to study our Benedictine Rule in more detail, especially the role of the abbot, the representative of Christ in our midst. I have always found it important to have a goal, so that my energies are concentrated in one direction; and I have come to realize that we gradually become what we love. So it is important that our love should have a worthy object and the only person supremely worth loving is Christ himself. So really the whole of our Christian endeavour is to come to know Christ and be transformed by that loving knowledge. Thus he is the Way to the Father and the Way to our fellow men.

I have probably gained much from spending almost the whole of my religious life so far in the novitiate! The contact with initially unformed minds – in the spiritual sense – and then the supportive role of novice mistress, have made me examine carefully and realistically what I really believe and what I try to live out. So personal responsibility and joyful acceptance of our interior freedom to choose what we become are dominant themes. For this, the old monastic concept of purity of heart is fundamental. We cannot have a pure heart if we do not have a clean mind, so one of our greatest needs is to fill our minds with what is good and laudable. It does not really matter if we do not retain what we have read, because the process of reading can cleanse the mind and leave it clean. I find an idea in Blosius helpful: his comparison of our minds to empty vessels which are filled with clean water and then rinsed out when we read and forget the content. So forgetting does not matter, but reading does.

For one who has suffered from acute periods of distraction during private prayer, the value of interior quiet is inestimable. Sometimes after battling in prayer for the entire half-hour, I have gone into the cloister and there been enfolded in peace. In one moment God can visit us and make all the foregoing struggle worthwhile. He does not depend upon our efforts, but we are entirely dependent upon him. I also remember the saying of a Jesuit retreat-giver, who stressed that we must not blame circumstances if we do not grow. We are not dependent upon circumstantial tranquillity but upon our own choice.

The liturgy, then, has been my chief source of nourishment, although probably more in the preparation than in the actual celebration. What I notice increasingly is the constant prayer that we may become receptive to what God offers, that God may recognize us as his children, that we may learn to love with our whole hearts. So I realize that I am part of a pilgrim Church which has not yet arrived but is struggling along. This makes sense and I know what it means to be always falling short yet wanting to go on. It also makes it easier to follow the practical guidance of St Benedict's Rule, especially chapter 4, 'The Tools of Good Works', and to value our vow of conversion of life.

These years of sharing with others, even two or three, have been enriching. I have come to realize how very much I have been given by nature and grace, as was once said to me. It is a joy to experience the complete truth of the saying: 'To him who has shall be given, and to him who has not, even what he thinks he has shall be taken away.' This contains a profound psychological truth. For most of my life I seemed to be a deprived have-not. Now that I have found inner freedom and joy I find that I am abundantly blessed, in every way. Everything is mine to share, and the more I share, the more there is to share. The friends I have made at every stage of my life remain friends and the relationship with many has deepened in joyousness. I have made many new contacts, often through letters which began as 'business', and nearly every member of the family I left behind in Germany has come into a closer relationship. But none the less there still remains the 'the still sad music of humanity', and the peace and joy have come only through the accepted pain and limitation of being a person in need of redemption, travelling along with others also only partially redeemed.

The time of my solemn profession, on the Feast of All Saints 1976, was profoundly happy. I had already been ten years in the religious life and so was quite sure of what I was doing. I wanted to be entirely consecrated to God in this way. During the ceremony, almost at the beginning, the nun who is to take solemn vows is engaged in a symbolic dialogue with the celebrant. Three times she is called to 'Come' and three times she responds, on each occasion moving nearer the sanctuary. She carries a lighted candle, symbolizing the faith granted her through the gift of baptism. The three summonses came to represent for me my three attempts to follow Christ in the religious life. Now the pact was to be sealed. I sang with deep conviction the words, 'Take me, Lord, to be your own according to your word, and I shall live. Let not my hope in you be disappointed.' And on my ring were inscribed in Latin the words 'Joy and hope', because my life had been enlightened by these gifts of the Spirit.

The knowledge that every strand of my life was coming together in that moment of personal dedication, that many, many people throughout the world were with me in spirit, made the whole ceremony meaningful beyond telling. I was borne up in spirit and during my three full days with sealed lips – perhaps the happiest of my life – I was conscious of a joyous welling-up in me that made me think of living water; and the silent murmur, 'Come to the Father' was quite insistent. I did not understand it, but was happy to be carried by the joyous peace.

I was now utterly convinced of the truth of our Lord's statement that he had come that we might have life and have it more abundantly. I had also realized that we are all potentially, if not actually, alienated people. Alienated from ourselves, from each other, from God. It is only the personal encounter with God's love, mediated by human beings, which can begin to free us. So my emphasis upon the grace of the present moment, which I had learned from de Caussade's *Abandonment to Divine Providence*, and found also in Marcus Aurelius, increased. It is only NOW that we live, only in this moment of time that we can love and respond. So the plea, 'O that today you would listen to my voice . . .' (Ps. 95 (94)) has great meaning for me. There is a wholeness and wholesomeness about Benedictine life at its best, and even discernible at its worst, which answers my deepest needs and aspirations.

I said at the beginning of my reflections that I have come to believe that any truly human experience is at least potentially a religious experience. There is nothing in the circumstances of our daily life which cannot bring us closer to God. But the key to all this is our own attitude. What we are like inside our own minds decides how we see and how we behave. So what matters is our inner being and surely the Beatitudes state this: 'Blessed are the clean of heart, for they shall see God.' I also said that I have learned that the old monastic striving for purity of heart is an essential means for attaining our goal of perfect love for God and man, and this imposes great discipline upon us. A pure or clean heart can only grow in us when our minds are clean, and most of us suffer from varying degrees of mental pollution. As I understand it, the simplest form of monastic life was designed as a practical help in our desire to learn to love God and to love our neighbour as ourselves.

The traditional monastic means for this are prayer in common and in private, spiritual reading, simple manual work in silence and a life lived in common. The needs of the individual in community are provided for and we are not subjected to rigid egalitarianism. To each one of us is, or should be, given according to our own individual need as long as this is not an intolerable burden to others. Our lifestyle is very simple. We have a small breakfast of bread and butter and tea. Monastic dinner consists of soup, a main course and some sort of dessert, often stewed apples in the winter. Supper consists of tea, bread and butter and jam, and something like cereal, or ham, the occasional egg or 'make-up' of left-overs from previous days. In the mid-morning we can have a mug of cocoa and there is tea in the afternoon. A recent welcome innovation has been sweets at recreation.

We have individual rooms called 'cells' in which we sleep, read and occasionally relax. There are no armchairs for the young and one soon gets used to hard wooden seats. The older nuns have wash-basins with running water in their cells, but the rest of us spread an old blanket on the floor and make our ablutions in an old tin bath or wash-bowl. We have proper baths, in a bathroom, twice a week.

So there is no luxury. In a small and ageing community finances are a constant worry. So we are encouraged to spend recreations and any free time in producing handicrafts suitable for sale in our small shop, and perhaps we emphasize the 'doing' rather than valuing the 'being' of our Sisters. But for most of us simple hand work is a form of relaxation and can be a creative activity.

Perhaps our assembling in choir at various intervals of the day, to dedicate those times explicitly to the love of God and to renew our own spiritual strength, is the greatest test of all. We have to be unselfish enough to drop the work we are engaged upon, however interesting, and go and be apparently 'unproductive' in church. We have to make the serious effort to empty our minds of our preoccupations and have the dispositions of the poor in spirit, empty of self, waiting on God. We have come to receive as much as to give. We have come to receive God's word in Scripture, to identify with the whole range of emotions expressed in the psalms and to pray accordingly. Sometimes the joy and praise echoes our mood; sometimes the anger, pain, vindictive-ness of the wronged express our anger and pain in community life. And sometimes it does not. But we are encouraged to pray with mind and voice in harmony, and every prayer at any time expresses the need of at least one human being somewhere in the world. This requires great faith and great self-discipline and often we fail miserably.

When I became a Christian, I knew that I had to lead a life in which everything mattered, in which I was totally engaged. This has been granted in the monastic life. We rise at 5.00 a.m. and have until the Morning Office at 6.15 to make our prayer in church, and to read. This period in church, early in the morning, is vitally important, even if tiredness and sleep linger and one is often drowsy. Breakfast follows on Morning Office an hour later. After that I am fully occupied until Mass. First we go to feed the cats who live a half-domesticated life in the outhouses and keep down vermin. Then we attend to the hens. The sheds have to be cleaned, and we now use wood-shavings in the nesting boxes, so for me there is the fleeting memory of the sawdust smell of early childhood. Without lingering, but glancing at the sea a mile away and having a quick look to see what is growing in the garden, we hurry back to the house. Ten minutes later I give a conference on the religious life or Scripture to the novitiate. That done, I hurry away to do my housework, which I just manage to finish before the last toll goes for Mass.

The morning is spent in the garden, or chicken-run, or in extra domestic chores. After Midday Office and monastic dinner, without any break, I go to my sewing room, where I work alone at making habits for various communities of Benedictine monks, as well as the occasional repairs for my own Sisters. Tea is followed by recreation, during which we often do light work or play 'Scrabble' in the novitiate. Then there is a period for prayer and reading before Vespers. Classes follow, or other work, before supper at 6.30 p.m. Compline ends the day and in the period before it I may have been able to take some time for preparing for the next conference, or just reading for enjoyment. So the day is full, and I am fortunate in having variety in my work and in being alone at work in the afternoons. That is a valuable breathing space, as I seem to need a fair measure of silence and solitude. I cannot help laughing inwardly when people wonder what enclosed nuns do all day. We have a house and grounds to maintain and need to earn something towards the expense of living, as well as retaining those essential periods of prayer in which we seek healing and forgiveness from God.

In the second retreat I heard from Abbot Hume, as he was then, he said jokingly but truly that in community we were all either 'crooks or crocks', to which we added 'cranks and creeps'. This means, of course, that it is not easy to live in community. So I have come to value increasingly St Benedict's injunction that the 'Our Father', is to be said aloud twice a day in the Office, because of 'the thorns of scandal which may arise'. This is by no means a new idea for me, because I needed forgiveness before I could come to accept myself and I still stand in constant need of it.

The gift of friendship is the greatest gift any human being can bestow on another, because it is the loving sharing of the most personal and intimate in one's being. But it can never be a total communion, as God alone has the key to the incommunicable in us; so in one sense we shall never be known by anyone except God. Yet love is a stimulus to growth and love freely given and freely received is the only incentive to constant reaching out; and we need human love to become ourselves. It is very freeing to be able to admit one's faults and failings without being judged, knowing that one is perhaps loved even more because one is vulnerable. With this acceptance comes the desire to respond more fully, to become more human with a heart of flesh and so perhaps a little less unworthy of love, human and divine.

Yet we need to learn what love is really all about. I found a key in the reverential awe in which Moses stood before the burning bush and I sympathized with Peter when he stepped back from the Lord, saying, 'Depart from me, for I am a sinful man'. There is much to reverence in human beings, as well as in God, so we need to become aware of the respect others deserve in their own right. This is what attracts me to the Rule of St Benedict, although most of the time I lack this reverence towards people and created things. Yet it is only through standing back and worshipping that we gain the gift of unpossessive love.

Through the small moments of awareness in my life I have come to appreciate the phrase 'the fear of the Lord'. I understand this as love and awe which want to serve and whose greatest joy is having the service accepted. During my monastic life I have often prayed for this gift of the Holy Spirit, as I also pray for wisdom. I can identify readily with the young Solomon as he dedicated the new temple, since I have now learned what he already knew. He knew that the greatest gift God can give us is forgiveness, because only when we have been forgiven and accepted in love can we turn outwards in love and acceptance of others. This was the basis of my key experience, surely a foreshadowing of the day when I shall finally stand before the face of God.

Since there is a wholeness about my present life and a constant awareness of being in God's presence, the fact that my periods of personal prayer are often far from inspiring does not seem to matter. I have long accepted my helplessness in this area and most of my moments of deepest peace come outside the time of 'prayer'. While grappling with the question of God's indwelling and our efforts at praying, I wrote the following:

> '. . . and let the questing mind be still . . .'
> In the ground of your being I have my home,
> so do not seek me in the world apart.
> Within your spirit true communion lies.
> You are no homeless stranger in a land afar,
> no alien on a foreign shore,
> for I am with you.
> Do but be still and know that I am God.
> I look upon the world with your dark eyes;
> I feel the flowing air on your cool cheek.
> I hear the twittering in the moving trees,
> for with your senses I perceive.
> I am with you, I am within you.
> So do not turn away but come to rest in me.
> Within you is our meeting place.
> Be but still, and I will speak in silence
> to your loving, wayward heart.

On a Human Note

DOM LEONARD VICKERS

It came as rather a shock and surprise when I was asked to join some other Benedictines of the English Congregation in drafting a book. We had been asked to consider aspects of our lives which might be helpful to others. Three of the team had already produced literary works. For me it was a completely new venture. I was soon to learn what a very hard task it is to put down clearly on paper thoughts which, when they are in your mind, seem so straightforward and full of meaning.

By January 1980 a number of contributions had come in from all the team and these had been passed round to other Benedictines and some lay people. It was felt that a great deal of the material might be of interest to monks and nuns, but not to the man in the street, whose experience and interests are often very different. The result was that five of the team wrote what might be called Odysseys: accounts of what had happened to them in their search for vocation and of the lessons they had learned in their lives. For a long time I felt that this was not for me; but with all the encouragement I received from the others and because I felt that I had learned so much from them, I decided in the end that I would discuss one or two of my own experiences.

When people ask me why I became a monk, I feel very like the engaged couple who are asked why they have fallen in love. We don't really know. What they *can* say, and I equally, is that certain things have happened to us in our lives which made us come to a decision. But very often when I am asked why I became a monk, what I am really being asked is: Why did I run away? Why am I trying to escape from real life? My only answer to this is that I don't think it is true. Nor do I feel that by becoming a monk I have made myself a prisoner, locked away from the world. Although I am only too aware that I don't deserve it, my time as a monk and later as a monk-priest has been a wonderful experience. There have been times, as I will explain later, when I have been tempted to pack up and leave and I expect there will be such times again in the future. But this is something which, as I have begun to understand, happens to most people: the grass can so often look greener on the other side. In reality my life in the monastery has been very exciting and fulfilled. I have learned a great deal from others, both inside and outside the monastery. All kinds of new opportunities have opened up for me, such as I never expected. Many wonderful and lasting friendships have been made; all kinds of people have allowed me to share their joys and sorrows, their happiness and their pain, in a way I would never have imagined. But perhaps this is jumping too far ahead.

In 1935, the year of my birth, my parents were living in India. I already had a brother three years older than myself who had been born there, but my mother had decided to return home for my birth and thus I was born in Belfast. For some reason (I have been told it was not because I was in danger of death) I was baptized the day after I was born. This has always intrigued me and I am sure it happens very rarely. I was given the baptismal names James Darragh, after my maternal great-grandfather. It was James Darragh who had started the family firm in India, having sailed there in 1855 from New York, where I presume he had gone to seek his fortune. But he soon realized the potentialities of coir fibre and determined to go to the country of its origin. He settled on the west coast of South India and was the first to instruct the people to spin yarn by the wheel instead of by hand. Tradition has it that he was so closely imitated by his operatives that they worked left-handed, even as Darragh did himself, he being, as they say in the States, 'south-pawed'.

My father had been born in Scotland, but on leaving school had joined James Darragh's firm and been sent to India. There he met my mother. It was her side of the family that in many ways would influence my early life most. Shortly after my birth, my father returned from India for good, to take over the London office. My maternal grandmother had been widowed early in life, and as there were no other children now left in Belfast, she came to live with us in our new home at Bromley, Kent. She was a very determined character who had lived a very full life, travelled a good deal, brought up seven children and loved to have priests (especially prelates) in the house, yet despite the great pride she had in herself she possessed a very simple faith and loved to go to daily Mass. From an early age my brother and I would accompany her, not from any motive of piety or holiness but because we were treated to ice-cream on the way home. All in all, she played a very prominent part in our life.

When I was four, the Second World War broke out. Since we lived quite near to Biggin Hill, the Battle of Britain air station, the bombing and air raids were severe, so it was decided that I should go at an early age to prep school. Alton Castle was in North Staffordshire and run by the Sisters of Mercy. The school was a castle built by the Earl of Shrewsbury on the site of an old castle which had been blown up by Cromwell. My years there were very happy; we were well taught and there were many extra-curricular activities such as art, drama, concerts and plays. The concerts and plays would often be put on for wounded troops. On one of these occasions we were doing *The Pirates of Penzance* and I was in the girls' chorus. When the pirates came we had to scream, 'Spare us!', I think it was three times, and take a step backwards. The third time I did this I stepped back too far and rolled down the steps at the side of the stage, ending up in the audience. It brought the house down. I don't know what the wounded troops were expecting; but I remember the one who kindly picked me up and lifted me on to the stage again, saying in a loud voice as he sat down, 'She's a boy'. The house roared again. There were also the happy times when we would have carol feasts, processing round the castle by candlelight, singing and ending up in the kitchens which were right at the bottom of the castle, what we called the dungeons. Here Sister Elizabeth would have prepared a feast and stories would be read to us.

Two men made a lasting impression on me at this time. One was the parish priest at Alton, Fr Samuel Gosling, who had been an army chaplain. It was the sermons he preached and his whole bearing that made him a hero in my eyes at the time. I also used to enjoy his sung Compline in English, which he quite often had on a Sunday evening. Years later I learned that it was Father Gosling who in 1942 convened a meeting for priests at Stanbrook Abbey, from which meeting grew up the English Liturgy Society, later known as the Vernacular Society. The other man was also a priest, Father Doran. He used to come down from Cotton College and teach us boxing. I had never seen priests doing things like this before and Father Doran was another hero.

Although I had been protected at Alton from many of the horrors of the war, my grandmother died in the summer holidays of 1943. When I went home she had already begun her final illness, which was to continue until the middle of August. Her death was a real shock to me and it was to be followed within two years by the death of my mother. A part of my life which only a short time before had seemed so secure and so full of love was suddenly taken away. We seemed to be suddenly bereft.

It was about this time, I think in the summer before my mother died and possibly because of her weak heart, that our family doctor suggested that I and my sister, who was three years younger, should go down to Cornwall. His daughter and her two children, about our ages, were staying with a relative at Stoke Climsland. I am sure if my grandmother had been alive she would have vetoed the suggestion, as it was at an Anglican vicarage that we were going to live. But for me it was a period of my life that I remember with great affection. Canon Martin Andrews was well known in Cornwall. My sister and I were just treated as part of the family. There was a farm attached to the vicarage, mainly market gardening, but I was taken milking, helped with the harvest and would often go to Evensong on a Sunday. This was my first experience of what my grandmother would have called the opposite camp, but Canon Andrews (at the time of writing he is still alive, aged ninety-five) has been a great inspiration to me in the matter of Church unity.

At this stage of my life the world I lived in seemed large and strange enough; I had already learned some lessons, but a great deal more still had to be learned. One experience I had in Cornwall taught me a valuable truth about passing judgement on others. Canon Andrews had also thrown open his vicarage to Australian Air Force officers who were convalescing from war wounds; a number of these were Catholics and I would get taken to Mass on the crossbar of a bike. I remember, the first time I was taken, being really frightened when we got to the church: about six or seven rows were occupied by Italian prisoners of war. 'Here', I remember thinking, 'are men who are surely wicked, who should not be in church. How can they love God when they have been fighting against my country?' Yet in the weeks which followed I was to discover that they were anything but that. They were as normal, loving and sincere as anyone else I had known. Obviously at the time it did not go any further than that. But now I realize that the reason they were in prisoner-of-war uniforms was that the war had been brought about not by God but by man. So often we judge people by what we think they are rather than by what they are in reality.

In 1946 I left Alton Castle and went to Douai. My schooling at Douai had been brought forward because the headmaster, Fr Ignatius Rice, felt that as my mother had died it would be better for my brother and me to be together. I was to be seven years in the school. By the time I reached the Sixth Form I had still not really decided what to do with my life. I had thought about Medicine and Law, but not seriously; in fact if anything I presumed I would join my father's firm and go out to India. One day in my last term one of the housemasters, Fr Norbert Bill, was taking up a collection for the foreign missions in the school refectory. When he came to my table he began asking people if they had ever thought of joining the monastery. 'There is great work to be done,' I remember him saying, and then: 'What about you, little man?' Everyone was addressed as 'little man', but he had nudged me. For some reason – I didn't know why at the time – I found myself saying, 'Yes, that might be an idea'. An interview was arranged with the Abbot and the Abbot saw my father.

My father was a very wonderful man. He had taught me over the years to try to be all things to all men. He certainly was so in his own life: he seemed to be at home with anyone. I think this was because he took an interest in people and what they were doing. Often my brother and I would walk down to the station with him in the morning or meet him in the evening. He was always interested in other people and their work: it could be the man sweeping the road, or the ticket collector, in fact just anybody: he had time for them and they too had time for him. He was an absolutely honest person, and even though I know my mother's early death caused him great sorrow he remained very young in heart. All our friends who came to our home found him very easy to relate to. The firm and his work meant a great deal to him and we would often tease him, saying that even when we were on holiday the firm would always be still in touch. Although all my education was at boarding schools, I treasure the time I was able to spend with my father.

Another person who also did a great deal for us children was our stepmother, Catherine, known to us as Auntie. My father had not remarried for a number of years, as he thought for a long time that we children would not want it. When he did, Auntie was a good stepmother and wife, but sadly the marriage lasted only seven years. My father died in 1955.

In September 1953 I became a novice. Many people might be amazed at this way of choosing a vocation. My feeling at the time was that during my seven years in the school I had almost come to look on Douai as a second home. I felt I had been given a great deal by all those involved with Douai and I hope I took up the challenge Father Norbert had put before me: 'There is great work to be done'. Looking back now, I realize there were many ways in which I did not mature. When we were sharing our papers in preparation for this book I felt, especially in reading the 'Jigsaw' and the 'Tapestry, from the Wrong Side', that in the development of my religious vocation I must have missed many experiences familiar to other young Religious. I had not experienced any real desert; I had never felt trapped or had torturous doubts to the extent that the others had. Things were done to curb my pride and make me more humble and detached, but I don't think I got the full spiritual benefit from them. I remember at my first Christmas being sent a table lamp and being told by the novice master that I could not have it. Instead of seeing in this the spiritual implications of detachment and the practice of poverty, I just wanted to pack up and go. At the time no one had left and I decided to put it off; I did not want to be the first.

One of the hardest things, I found, was being cut off from one's friends outside. You could write home each week, but you did not get home for four years. The novices were also kept separate from the rest of the community, being with them only on what was called a 'Month Day' (a day off once a month) and the periods set aside for holidays in the summer and at Christmas. I think that, apart from that time at Christmas, what kept me from leaving was the attitude we had been taught: stiff upper lip, grin and bear it, and all that. Certainly another major help was that in my first year as a novice there were eight of us in the novitiate and at the start of the second year twelve. To some extent it was us against 'him', the novice master, and although we knew that he would always win, there were enough of us to support each other. Many of the methods of training we then experienced have since been done away with. Some of them were removed in the renewal that has taken place in religious life and some because the novitiate is now very much smaller. Nowadays, novices are a little older when they join. They are not cut off from their families to the extent that we were, nor from the rest of the community, and their life is better integrated into what they will be doing for the rest of their lives. Yet I am sure that in these first years there is still testing enough to discover whether the novice is 'truly seeking God', as St Benedict requires in his Rule.

One job I began in the novitiate continued for six years; its performance and responsibilities brought out in me a side I never knew existed. In those days there was a great deal of outdoor activity: orchards, chickens, the grounds and the pigs. I was allotted the pigs and soon became very engrossed in the pig farm. This was surprising, as I knew nothing about them when I began. We had breeding sows and pigs which we fattened for pork and bacon. Unusually for a novice, I was allowed to do the marketing, keep the accounts, arrange vet visits and the buying of the food. The herd had to be fed twice a day, swill had to be cooked and the sties kept clean. My involvement with the farm made me wonder, just before my final vows, if I should become a Cistercian. My confessor and spiritual director assured me that it was not for me; in fact he roared with laughter. He was absolutely right and knew me better than I knew myself. I had simply equated the Cistercian life with a monastic life in which the monks farmed; but there is much more to it than this and if I had not listened to my director I am sure I would not have lasted long in a Cistercian monastery.

A lesson I was to learn at this time was that when I thought my life was going in one direction, the Abbot and his council set it off in another. I was ordained priest in 1960 and at the time I was sure that I would be going up to Oxford to read History. But in 1961 the community received a severe blow in the death of Fr Anthony Baron, the Bursar. I was asked to become Assistant Bursar and because of this had to give up the teaching I had been doing in the school. At the time I felt a certain amount of impoverishment. On the first day in the new job I was asked to unpack and store various supplies that had been delivered and I remember thinking to myself, 'Is this what I have been ordained for?' How wrong I was. Because I was free of classes I was soon asked to help Fr Oswald Dorman, the parish priest of the surrounding parish, which had been growing quite rapidly. Father Oswald had taken it over at the age of sixty-five after a life's work in the school. In his twelve years as parish priest he built four churches and fostered a parochial community which in many ways reflected the teaching of the Second Vatican Council. I will always be grateful for the training he gave me as his curate.

When I joined the monastery, the Douai community consisted of about eighty-four monks. A great many of these were serving on the various parishes which we had in England and Wales. Over the years some of these men retired back to the monastery and brought back with them a great wealth of experience. Some had served in parishes in mining areas, or in big city parishes such as Coventry. They had had the care of large hospitals, both general and mental, and they had experienced many of the tragedies of the war. Their wisdom and counsel, their example of detachment, were a powerful reminder that external results are not the measure of the value of monastic life and work. They were then and are still a great asset to the monastic family. I feel there is a lesson in this for society today: I am sure family life would be very much enhanced if we were to retain and care for the elderly more within the family. I know that for many this may seem very hard and most of the structures of society today are against it. I remember a warden of a very well-run and well-appointed home for the elderly telling me that when newcomers arrived the family would often show great interest. But it made him sad to notice that their visits, at first very regular, would tail off until they ceased altogether. I know that many are working at this problem within our society. One very good step has been to build bungalows for the elderly within the complex of an estate, instead of just grouping a whole lot together. In this way those who live in them do not feel so cut off, for they see life and activity going on around them, which helps them greatly. It is also heartening to see many 'Good Neighbour' schemes and the like springing up within various communities.

In many ways I think that at this time in my life I felt I was getting the best of both worlds: serving as a priest in the local parish at Burghfield and yet living in the monastery. For the next twenty years I was on the local parish and I am sure I received far more from those I served than I gave them. It was a wonderful life and I learned many lessons. In pastoral work I discovered how generous people were in receiving me into their homes; they shared so many of their joys and sorrows and I found great happiness and spiritual help in the celebration of the sacraments, especially in offering the Mass. Together with all this, I soon realized what great support I could get from so many of the monks in the monastery. We used to tease Father Oswald that he had seventeen curates; but in actual fact I had them as well.

Monks are really no different from the rest of mankind and one thing I discovered at this time was that I was going through the external motions of prayer, but not really praying. As a result I seemed to draw no closer to God. I think many people have this experience. It is what Fr Simon Tugwell in his book on prayer calls the two dangers: 'In our relationship with God, one of the main problems is that half the time we just forget about it . . . Habits must begin somewhere. And just where we need to build up good habits is often precisely the occasion where we simply forget all about it' (Simon Tugwell, OP, *Prayer, Keeping Company with God*, vol. i, pp. 3, 4). Yes, this was me. My life as a monk was habit-forming: the routine of the day is divided into periods in which one is brought to God's house so that one does not forget God. And yet even here there were dangers. Unless one turns oneself consciously to be aware of the prayer, the praise and the worship one is offering and unless one forms good habits rather than just habits, so much of one's time is spent in merely going through the motions of prayer and, in my case, through the motions of monastic life as well. What happened to me and brought about an understanding of the difference between 'just habit-forming' and 'good habit-forming' was that in the early 1970s there seemed to grow up within the Church as a whole, and also in the monastery, a response to the call for renewal. We were asked to take a good hard look at ourselves, at the way we were living our lives and at the fullness of that life. I soon discovered that in order to get more out of my life I had to put more in, that the whole relationship with God was a two-way relationship.

On a human level one can often understand better and see more easily how relationships are formed. I remember listening to the funeral service of Lord Louis Mountbatten. For a number of days prior to this a great deal had been written in the press about him. But what struck me most was that so many people from all walks of life and from all age groups held him in such high esteem. I am sure the reason for this was that here was a man who had communicated with others and others had felt they could communicate with him. So whether it was his closeness to the Royal Family, or the esteem felt by his many friends who had served with him during the war, or the links he had formed in his own area of Hampshire with people from every walk of life, what it came down to was that Lord Mountbatten had communicated with them and made them feel completely at home with him. In other words, he had responded and formed relationships. This reminded me very much of my father. The same is true with God. Men and women who are searching for God in their lives should realize that this relationship is possible. It is not being a monk, a priest or a Religious that makes it so. It is a matter of response, of both giving and receiving.

Another reason why I think the death of Lord Mountbatten made such an impact on me was that I had met him on a visit he made to HMS *Dauntless*, the training establishment for girls who are joining the WRNS. On that occasion he had come to take a passing out parade and when he met the Wrens and their parents afterwards I noticed what a wonderful rapport he immediately had with them. It was the same when he came to the wardroom for tea. When he spoke to you, you got the impression that you mattered and that he was interested. HMS *Dauntless* was part of our parish and in 1966 I was asked to become an officiating chaplain. This meant that every Friday I spent the day taking Religious Education classes for all the Catholics who spent their first four weeks in the Wrens at HMS *Dauntless*. Full-time chaplains in the forces normally get drafted about every two years, but an officiating chaplain stays put. In the eleven years I went to *Dauntless* I made many friends among these girls and learned from them a great deal about Religious Education throughout the British Isles. The regulations that were laid down when I started there were excellent: all the girls joining had to come to the Chaplain's Hour, as it was called. The Navy regarded the Church as part of naval life and it was part of my job to let the girls know what the chaplain's role was. I discovered that many people are really looking for God in their lives. It was sad that so many of the girls had drifted away from the official Church because they had not found a caring Church. Many of them had never really spoken to a priest; they often saw him as just a distant figure and sometimes as rather a fierce person. Service life was the first opportunity they had had to discuss their problems in a relaxed way.

There were two other aspects of Service life that I found most helpful. The first was working with chaplains from the other denominations. I remember that on my first day at HMS *Dauntless* the Church of England chaplain had been assigned to take me round the establishment and introduce me to all the various sections: sick bay, main deck, galley, new entry and so on. He could not have been kinder or more helpful. This is one of the wonderful things about Service life: the chaplains I have met always seem to have such a good relationship with each other. A great many of the interchurch barriers were not present in the Royal Navy.

The second great help I got was from the Roman Catholic chaplains. When I became an officiating chaplain, Mgr George Pitt was the Senior Catholic Chaplain. Each year he would invite me to the Chaplains' Week that was held in London. During the week we would discuss our work and listen to guest speakers. Over the years I got to know a great many of the chaplains and made many lasting friendships.

It was this link which led to my involvement in moral leadership courses, as they are called, which were started first of all in the Portsmouth area, then in Plymouth and also in Scotland. These have now grown into a very rewarding activity. Just how rewarding is best described by a report that was written up by Patrick O'Donovan in the *Catholic Herald*. He has kindly let me quote it and I do so because it says so much about the Church today. He called it 'Great Oaks in the Making'.

> If news were about great and good things this, like a processional cross, would have led the paper. But being what it is, it is tucked away in a corner of the Charterhouse cloister. I went last week to the Pastoral Centre for the diocese of Portsmouth. They were holding one of their periodic RN moral leadership weekends. The young men and women, with a few from schools, came from a Friday afternoon to a Sunday evening for a course in their Faith . . .

There was an atmosphere of the most extraordinary gaiety about this isolated house. There was horseplay in the corridors and attention at the lectures and no apparent observance of rank. The young men who predominated looked on the whole tough and abominably healthy. The girls were pleasing and considered themselves equals. There was a considerable course of lectures. One lot was given by Ursula Fleming who studies pain.

So strike me, she was telling these young sailors how to pray. She is a sturdy, handsome lady. She was dressed in trousers and a fisherman's smock and she was telling them about posture. But somehow she had got them to shed their conventional inhibitions. She sat and murmured to a room full of them, got them to take their shoes off and balance broom sticks on their fingers as an exercise in concentration, taught them to sit at attention when in Church, taught them to rise for the Gospel, breathing in as they did so, without breaking the concentration and no one mocked. As she went on, telling them not to call the Mass 'boring' or to judge the performance of the priest as if he were a performer, they listened with interest and without awe. She got them to genuflect balancing the broom stick and then to do the same without. She was getting them to involve their all in their prayers. And her rapport with these young people was gentle and entertaining and quite unforced.

The other speaker was Dom Leonard Vickers, a youngish Benedictine priest from Douai. He had them hard at work thinking for themselves about things they had taken for granted, about the liturgy, about what is the Church, about the natures of human and divine. And they worked at it in groups as if it were exciting. No concessions were made to them and the subjects could have stumped the most rarefied Newman Society. They had discos in the evening and a bar and bare discipline expressed in naval terms, like 'pipe down' for 'lights out'.

But the climaxes on Saturday and Sunday were the Masses in the spare, modern church at Park Place. They came in chatting and then seemed utterly to commit themselves. Now I contradict everything I have written here before. Everything I profess to dislike was done. There were guitars and a folk Mass called the Israeli Mass and it was marvellous and naturally intense. When it came to the bidding prayers, one of them prayed for a friend up on a murder charge. When it came to the liturgy of the Eucharist, everyone stood packed around the altar. They joined hands and swayed to sing the Our Father. And when it came to the Kiss of Peace a sort of joyous riot broke out. The boys kissed the girls, gently. There was a milling about to shake hands. At least two young men said to me: 'Peace be with you – Sir!' Sunday Mass was at midday after a morning of work. When it was over they opened the bar. But most of them stayed behind to sing hand-clapping hymns for the fun or something else of it.

Perhaps there is something special in the community spirit of the Royal Navy. Perhaps these were the special ones left after all the lapsed Catholics had dropped off the tree. I, myself, have never seen anything more hopeful for the future of the Church. And the people who chose to come and to participate without mockery or tedious embarrassment, some looked like tough nuts, some looked and sounded intellectually deprived, some seemed to be people for whom the sky is the limit. All together, they looked like the future.

Perhaps this is rather a long statement to put in a piece such as this. But for me Patrick O'Donovan has summed up in his wonderful turn of phrase much of what I see the Church should be about. The only thing he was wrong about is that many of those present were not 'the special ones left after all the lapsed Catholics had dropped off the tree'. Many had been well and truly lapsed, but had come back because they have truly found Christ again through contact with their chaplains and their helpers. Since these courses were started some years back, groups of eight at a time have also come up and spent weekends in the monastery at Douai. They have come to all the monastic prayer in choir, they eat and take their recreation with the community and very often help with work that is being done. They have often told me how much they have enjoyed the silence as well as everything else and how when they came for the first time they had no idea it would be so; in fact often they have told me that they were a little frightened and apprehensive.

In 1970 I became parish priest, Fr Oswald Dorman having retired because of ill-health. It was almost a very short term of office. One day I was driving Father Abbot back from Worth Abbey; we were just rounding a rather sharp bend when the Abbot suddenly said, 'What about you becoming novice master?' We almost ended up in the ditch. Whether it was the scare I gave him or the shock he realized it gave me, the matter was not raised again until 1977. In the interim period of grace, or whatever one calls it, I was to be involved in the building of a new church at Burghfield. Up to this time we had been using a dual-purpose church hall. The parish had now grown considerably and I derived a great sense of fulfilment from yet another new venture. My paternal grandfather had been an architect sculptor and although I myself had never shown any artistic talent it was sheer joy to be closely associated with architects, but especially with the artists, sculptors and craftsmen who designed the church and its furnishings. Many of these people have a wonderful sense of creativity, are gentle and seem to be at peace with themselves and their world. Most of them were local craftsmen and I found it a deeply spiritual experience to share their thoughts and see them developed and then taking shape in the church itself.

In 1977, I did become novice master. This time Father Abbot did not ask me in a car, but after a council meeting. Outsiders often think that monks are just told to do things by the Abbot and that is that. But St Benedict lays down in his Rule that an abbot should take counsel from the other members of the community. I find this helpful. Often too in my monastic life, when I have been asked to take on a new job, I have felt unable to do it; but then the community steps in and gives me help and encouragement. It happened with this Odyssey, which I almost called 'Late Starter', because the rest of the group had nearly finished theirs. I had decided there was no real story for me to tell, until after all manner of kindnesses from the others and a final note in the minutes of a meeting: 'Father Leonard's hoped-for Odyssey?', I began. I got the same support from my own community when I became novice master. Father Abbot would sometimes say to me when I had had some very enjoyable parochial experience, 'Now make sure, Leonard, the parishioners are worshipping God and not worshipping you.' Many a word of truth is spoken in jest. I know I often felt it was the latter and enjoyed it. Seventeen years in one parish for a young priest is unusual. I loved the work and loved the people. I know the Abbot realized that I would find the change in work difficult to adjust to, as he very kindly let me retain the Woolhampton part of the parish, which softened the blow.

Now after three years as novice master I can say that I have found the new work very rewarding too. In many ways I felt that I was beginning my monastic life again with my first novices. I have learned a great deal: I have enjoyed taking them for the study of the Rule, the psalms and all the other things that novices have to learn. At times they must have wondered what I was doing with them. On one occasion I was using a tape by Ursula Fleming on how to relax in order to concentrate. It was to put over how we must learn to be still, and my idea was to apply it to prayer. The tape required that those using it should lie down flat on the floor and then relax throughout the body. I thought it would be a good idea to do it with the novices; but by the time the tape had ended the novice master had relaxed so well that he had fallen asleep. The novices told me afterwards that they were not sure if they should let me be or wake me up. They took the latter course and then also let me know that I snored. It was later that I was to meet Ursula Fleming for the first time at Park Place. She was amused to hear what had happened, but added that she was also very pleased.

But what this most recent period of my life seems to have done for me is to make me realize that if I really wish to discover my wholeness, if I really desire the right balance to life, I cannot do it by myself. No human dynamics, no amount of good will can create and sustain our response to the demands of living a Christian life. I think St Paul's words to the people of Corinth are beginning to sink in: 'Examine yourselves to make sure you are of the Faith. Test yourselves. Do you acknowledge that Jesus Christ is really in you? If not, you have failed the test.'

In September 1980 I was asked to take over another new Douai venture, the running of a lay community. The spadework had been done by another monk, Father Finbar. In the short time since then, the seventeen young men and women who are weekend members and the first three residents seem to have given me more than I have given them. I have found in them a selfless dedication to others, a quest for prayer and a desire to experience real Christian living. When we fall back on ourselves and forget the trust, hope and love that Christ has given us, we remain stunted and grow sour; when we are open to the kind of development that brings about vigorous growth in understanding, knowledge and wisdom, we become more whole.

Reflections

Before I entered the monastery I was interviewed by the novice master. One of the questions he asked me was, had I read the Rule of St Benedict? I had to admit that I hadn't. He seemed rather shocked at this and suggested that I should do so. I never got round to it before entering. I don't know if I would have gleaned very much at that time, but now I have begun to realize what a masterpiece it is. When I have tried to escape from St Benedict's teaching by not listening, or have tried to escape from 'the toil of obedience by the sloth of disobedience', things have never really been right. The Rule is called the Rule because it guides straight the lives of those who obey.

In recent years obedience, which is so central in St Benedict's teaching, has had a bad press. For some people the word is another name for spinelessness or the immaturity of those who shirk responsibility in making decisions. For others it does not necessarily suggest lack of maturity, but conjures up the image of an army or any large organization, where discipline and conformity are demanded and the needs or preferences of individuals take second place. To vow oneself for life to what is known as a 'total institution', in which obedience pervades the whole of existence, seems to many people an abdication of human dignity and therefore abhorrent.

As I see things now, it seems to me that it is because these views on obedience prevail so much in our society that so many people today find their lives rather empty and meaningless. But I have to admit that when I embarked on my monastic life I may well have had a very jejune notion of obedience. For me it meant doing what I was told. It was therefore difficult to see why it was regarded as so significant: necessary, yes, but a functional necessity, not something to be blown up into a great issue. But now I see it as something far wider and more total than this. A life of obedience involves:

> A single-minded determination to go on, to say Yes, to refuse nothing.
>
> A sense, therefore, of unity and simplicity: this in a life that is often multiple and fragmentary.
>
> A lot of bafflement, humbling self-knowledge, disillusion, awareness of failure and inner poverty.
>
> Being treated far more tenderly, gently and generously than I ever bargained for.
>
> Being given great joy, a consciousness of broadening horizons and of fuller life at the price of many deaths.
>
> An awareness that all these mysteries are found at their highest power in my union with Christ.

In my case all this has come about because I am a monk. But obedience in its depth and fullness is not a monastic prerogative at all; it is, for instance, characteristic of the relations between husband and wife in a happy marriage. I feel that obedience is so primary and fundamental that it is equally characteristic of Christian life in any context and indeed of all truly human life.

When St Benedict wrote his Rule he was trying to build up a spiritual family. He wanted his monks to be content and find fulfilment. But these are everybody's goal: what St Benedict said holds good for all family life, for parents, for children, for society as a whole. Obedience is our response and we can often be clearer about its nature if we think of it as 'acceptance'. What I have had to learn at many different stages in my life is that I must:

> Accept my being and life from my Creator as a gift and a task.
>
> Accept my individual make-up, my calling and responsibility.
>
> Accept other people in their individuality, and the work or growing into human relationships with them.
>
> Accept my family, community or the group to which I belong and the wider family of all mankind.
>
> Accept the people with whom I work and share in the common effort.
>
> Accept the increasing mysteriousness of God in my life, and the inner solitude and poverty that there must be, if I am to let him be God for me.
>
> Accept his self-gift to me in love, his affirmation of me, his forgiveness and his creative word that gives me meaning.
>
> Finally, I must accept my own weakness and limitations.

As I reflect on my life so far, I realize that there is still a great deal more acceptance needed in it. When the 'I, I, I, Me, Me, Me' comes into my life (that is what my grandmother used to say to us children when we wanted our own way) I know I am not accepting my life as God's gift. There are times when I have not accepted my individual make-up, when I have not been faithful to my calling and when I have shirked responsibility. At all the stages in my life I have found it much easier to relate to those I like. But I am glad that acceptance of others also requires the work of growing. As can be seen from what I have written, I have been extremely fortunate in the love I have received from my family and the acceptance I have found from my monastic community and the parishioners in my pastoral work. Hence my acceptance of them has been comparatively easy. Now that the media brings the rest of the world so close, I realize that I still have to work very hard in my acceptance and also my awareness of the wider family of mankind.

I do find God's ways mysterious. Sometimes I am frightened. When I see suffering, pain, bafflement, disillusion, rejection, misunderstanding and injustice in the world around me, I sometimes wonder. But then I find great comfort in words such as St Augustine wrote in one of his sermons: 'The passion of our Lord Jesus Christ gives us the confidence of glory and a lesson in the endurance of suffering.'

What of my weakness and limitations? I have often gone wrong. I am sure many have been hurt by what I have said and the way I have behaved. But if I can bring acceptance into my life, I will, in the words of St Benedict, 'have put nothing whatever before Christ, and he in his turn will bring me and all of us to life eternal'.

Monastic Malcontent

DOM FABIAN GLENCROSS

My monastic Odyssey is not quite the edifying tale of the other contributors to this book. Their happiness shines through like members of a ship's company under a good captain. I was, even as a boy, the sort of person who hid in a barrel and ate green apples; as a man, the sort of official who quickly became first mate and thought of mutiny. It has been my fate to stumble constantly into the wrong camp; my life has been a continuous political campaign, full of chaos and muddle. It was as if even the 'black patches' I handed out to the crew (and there have been more than a few) were made of Bible paper and had the opposite of the intended effect. My Odyssey finds me still at sea and in far waters on the coast of Peru: still sailing, still lost, still grumbling at my Long John Silver-haired superior for his buoyancy and confidence, for being one-eyed and lame. Mine has been a very difficult life for other people.

My family has never seemed to me to be quite ordinary. We were eleven and I the youngest, with six strongminded sisters between me and my brothers. Of them, Kitt was hag-ridden by accountancy examinations, Roger away in Aden with the RAF and Nick a seminarist in France. The Glencrosses were a monolithic and matriarchal tribe. When I first read *Erewhon*, the stone figures seen through the mist and making hollow sounds through their ever-open mouths were no surprise to me: they could only be the family. And there they stand to this day, slightly lichen-grown with age, but still gigantic and vociferous; though one, Roger, fell for his country in May 1940.

Both my parents were the children of Cornish parsons and both parents converts to Catholicism. My father was near blind and largely, blissfully, unaware of the politics and strife of family life. He was a genealogist of some note and Fellow of three of the relevant societies; a very studious man who spent his time reading, even fourteenth-century script, but he left living mostly to his wife. My mother was blessed with incredible energy and marvellous devotion. She would start her Wimbledon day by bicycling through the dark to the 6.00 a.m. Mass in the Jesuit church on the Ridgeway and finish the day writing up to five letters to her far-flung family.

My parents became Catholics – though it was well before my time – because they believed in duty and structure. They had lost confidence in the Church of their fathers because they felt Anglicanism had lost consistency, lost really its sense of discipline. The Catholicism which grew in the house was typically that of converts: loudly anti-Protestant, strongly devoted to Benediction and a highly moralistic and hierarchic society. This sense of structure was also present in our 'county' background. Uncle Harry reigned as squire of the country house outside Bodmin; Granny at ninety-two still held sway; Aunt Maud and Great Aunt Constance stalked Bath in purple hats and satin chokers: all English in every inch and gentle stock to boot.

Our family, a little Cornish subculture, lived its jungle existence in the Worple Road, Wimbledon, and in the parish of the Sacred Heart. We were visited by some excellent unknown Jesuits from the college up the hill, and there, after a year or two with the Ursulines, I was intended to be educated. I hoped from my earliest years to be some day a Jesuit there. But one day, at the tender age of seven, unwarned, unable to read, dyslexic and lisping, I was taken to Wimbledon College and led down long corridors and left in the room of a tight-lipped, thin and elderly Jesuit. Under the interrogation I was no hero and as a result he found me lacking. The Glencross plans, as was usual and amid a chaos of feminine comment, had gone wrong again.

It was no surprise to me; I did not trust the adult world in which the individual had little value. It imposed a structure on me, using all the stock phrases of a deeply conservative outlook. What I came to understand of this adult edifice, I came to obey as the only source of value, as an object of loyalty and sometimes as a refuge. There were, for instance, moments when lack of energy made it comfortable to conform to the behests of my society; to be a 'good little boy', though physically a highly dangerous political stance to take amid my *realpolitik* sisters, was none the less a relief on occasion. Yet the real world was not with the structure but with the tiring, incessant strife between people. In Graham Greene's *A Sort of Life* he says that in his home (his father was a headmaster) the house was divided by a green baize door: on one side, the tranquil garden and the odour of his mother's perfume; on the other, the real world of the school with its smell of ink and touch of violence. 'Home' for me, all these years, has been one structure or other; but I can never explain my monastic life at

Downside, at Worth, at San Benito de Las Flores, unless I can make it clear that I have often found myself on the violent side of the door, sometimes creeping back to enjoy the comforts, but quickly sickened by the perfume and the laziness and cowardliness of it. Perhaps that grim shadow of a Jesuit long ago understood too well my fierce refusal to speak to him.

The immediate result of my failure at the hands of the Jesuits was that at the tender age of eight I was sent away to a non-snob boarding school, the John Fisher School near Croydon, only five miles from home and a single bus ride from Wimbledon. My parents visited the school only once in four years. I found myself therefore in the real world indeed. And there too I met those ubiquitous powers, the priests. One of them (though you won't believe me) beat me every day for six months; and another, while I was yet only ten, introduced me to Keats. It was a fine school in real living and of course I hated it. All this time the desire or decision to be a priest persisted. I began to follow my mother's norm of daily Mass, and Religious Instruction became a serious matter to me. The priest who beat me could no longer reach me, as I served the headmaster's Mass as an altar boy; nor was he likely to kill me for bad RI. I enjoyed the detailed metaphysics and exact casuistry of the time. Here, I believed, was the clue, the key to the door of the structure; theology had the cleanness and truth of mathematics and with a bit of effort I would find out what it was that the adults put their value in. Religious Instruction was about something that really mattered, an alternative to the real world I found so harsh. It talked of a world of saints and a life of purity and logic. It would be a strict world perhaps but one – perhaps the only one – in which one could be truly honest.

On the other side, I was shown a world of sin, quite a different world from the world of metaphysics or the real world I knew so well. Sin had nothing to do with the struggle between people, the forming of groups, the fighting, the theft: it was chiefly concerned with unpunctuality, talking in prep, drinking a drop of water before Communion. But in a way this new structure, this pre-war Catholic morality, was a marvellous thing: every detail, every gnat was weighed and strained away. Oh, to be a pharisee, to know all the law and get it right: I loved it. Priesthood seemed more and more the only hope I had of finding my way out of my real jungle and into an honest world. As I got older and sexual images began to dart across the shadows, I became more and more concerned to be honest, 'good' and clean. So it was that as I finished my four years there, I gradually lost my resilience against the local oppressor, the priest who had always beaten me, and I began to slip into a dull conformity and rank cowardice. The adults began to say how much I had improved. In fact I was looking for a life that would be right and clean and would lead me out of the real world of sin and sweat. For the first time I experienced muddle. Real life was a jungle to be avoided; the world of sin, which I fell into from time to time, racked me with scruples; the holy world, the structure, was too 'pi', so cowardly that to lead such a life made me ashamed. When I became a priest, I would know my way out of this muddle, I thought.

I was rescued from this new strife by the arrival of German bombers, first at Croydon and then at Wimbledon. I experienced the excitement and then the boredom of danger during those blitz nights. So my parents decided that two sisters and I should go to Cornwall to our Harris-tweeded uncle and that I should go to school away in Hereford. Thus I lived two years of what for my ancestors had been a norm. I played cricket in a country meadow among the cows and was driven in the headmaster's rickety vehicle to church every Sunday. There was a school structure, of course, and there was the inevitable tough boys' underworld, but the adults tried to make their students happy and largely succeeded. Hugh Arbuthnott, the headmaster, came also of a huge Catholic family and one that wore its Catholicism like a tailor-made coat, with ease and style. I began to experience something for which I have always been grateful: a Catholicism rich in beautiful things and built around extraordinary, often eccentric characters. Never again could I look on the intricate mechanism of pre-war morality, the weighing out to the last gram of the fast-day breakfast, the fear of drinking even a teaspoonful of water before Communion, except with humour or as a simple task to be done. This little school educated my conscience and led me out of the bourgeois world. Not that this growth did not in its own way falsify my vision; it was years, perhaps decades, before I realized it. I had stumbled into an aristocratic world where one's happiness in, and loyalty to, a class and a form of leisure made any other way of life seem less worthy and slightly ridiculous. To be English and to be Catholic were both heritages I had long ago used to support my good and clean structure; and now was added another strut: a sense of style.

In 1942 I moved across the Severn to Downside and quickly found myself in another and greater structure. Again I was back in a world where priests were the most important people in society: they represented authority, they punished, they award-ed, they taught everything—English, Latin, rugby and boxing. Not only was the monastic community the foundation on which all value was built, but it had that style which previous structures lacked. Also, it had embedded in it part of my family history which I had never known. A Downside monk of proven eccentricity, Dom Maurus van Thiel, had converted my mother twenty years before; a whole generation of monks had been at school with my three brothers at Ealing Abbey, a daughter house of Downside, in the 1920s and early 1930s. So Downside had a wealth of family and monastic history to offer; fairly soon I knew that I would try to make it my home by becoming a monk there at the end of my schooling, if the war and fighting did not stop me. I did not, of course, understand at the age of fourteen how the monks could spend so long in choir or put up with so much Latin; nor did I understand, though it was a constant interest to me, what motives lay behind the presence in the school and monastery of just these very unusual people. I began to be astounded at Catholicism and for the first time a sense of wonder arose in me. It was not a disbelief but an awareness, after years of conscious piety, of my ignorance of the richness of Catholicism. And there came, as is my wont, an amusement at watching other people covering up their ignorance; for a quantity of acid has always been part of the mixture in my character.

But again I was back in the real world and a harsher and more complicated world it proved than I had expected or experienced before. What I encountered for the first time on entering the underworld at Downside School was 'class'. It was not the class of the outside world, we were all much of a muchness; but I had broken the normal rules and found myself advanced to the 'second year' where I did not belong. In our underworld and sometimes in the monastic structure, where you came in the five-year system was the basic reality; if you transgressed the social norms, as a few of us were forced to do, you were without friends or allies for years. And criss-crossing the social world were other forces. It was a world I knew and although I found it painful I participated in it with some relish; but it is not a hades I like to remember. The thieving, the deep and grim rivalry between house and house, the rumours and reality of love between boys was a Dickensian picture I would rather not have with me. In fact, of course, there was little sin, but as we did not realize this, conscience was a corrosive power. Hence it was the confessional that became an escape hatch against the incoming sea. The structural world of the priests never touched our underworld, but in the darkened anonymous box they listened in on our mutterings. I did not go to the confessional to get any help in the social conflict or to be put right in my sexual turmoil; to ask for help would have been useless and cowardly. Socially and sexually you had your own place; it was all quite simple: you had to keep your square. The confessional put you back on the right part of the grid, until relentlessly you were blown off course again and you had to return to the pilot in his box.

Strangely, love was not part of the approved monastic structure, but it was very much part of the stress and joy of the underworld. In the Downside storms I lived through, it was quite acceptable to be passionately committed to someone older or younger, someone on quite a different square, or even off the Downside chart altogether; but love was like smoking, a mere diversion. Those early Downside years were extremely complicated, but not without joy. I moved into a rugby and boxing group, but also into my first experience of music and ubiquitous reading. As the muscles grew, so the social conflicts diminished and I became more and more part of the social norm, until my perspicacious sisters when they met me called me mockingly 'our Downside boy'. I look with loathing now on that adolescent figure with its unacceptable face of class snobbery. I was confident on my social square, a little higher now than some others, but in my heart I suffered the pangs of conscience that I could not keep my sexual square. But that would be put right when I entered the monastery and learnt the mysteries of the sea.

The war ended just as I was leaving school. I would have become a soldier along with my generation but for a stray question Dom Edmund Lee, my housemaster, asked me in my last month at school. It produced the answer, if I remember rightly, 'I would not mind joining the monastery'. So again I found myself walking down long religious corridors to visit a gaunt and to me elderly priest. But Abbot Trafford was no studious academic and I came trailing clouds of glory. I had rugby colours and a bruised face from boxing, so my academic laziness and basic incompetence were overlooked without a word. I enjoyed the visit and liked what I thought at the time was a simple man. I found I shared a view with this friendly Olympian: join a first-rate regiment with a long history and a good colonel and all would be well. So it was that at the age of just eighteen I marched into the monastery at Downside in February 1946; I was slightly frightened, but I was quite clear that this was where I should be and where I would stay for the rest of my life. It never occurred to me to look back or think of going back 'to the world'; just occasionally I had the experience my fellow novice John Roberts (now Abbot of Downside) put so neatly: 'I wish someone would throw me out of this place.'

I was brought up to believe, having learnt history as part of my patriotism, that the Punjab did not join the Indian Mutiny in 1858 because the colonel in charge beat his sepoys so hard and imposed such a rigid discipline on his troops that they all *loved* him and so remained loyal and good. It was with much the same sense of discipline that I joined Dom Alban Brooks's first novitiate. We were his first command after the war and ex-naval chaplain Brooks meant all to be shipshape. No doubt the discipline was not all that different from what generations of Benedictine novices had accepted with zest for centuries: up at 5.00, three hours of prayer before breakfast, sung High Mass daily, four hours of study, two hours of manual labour, two more hours of spiritual exercises and then bed at 9.00 p.m., completely tired. We were under a rule of silence for all but two hours a day; and forbidden to talk to women, lay people and all members of the community except, in theory, the Abbot and, very much in practice, the novice master. Our society consisted of six people: an ex-naval officer, an ex-prisoner of war, a middle-aged priest, one contemporary from the same rugby team, myself and, of course, the captain of the ship. The harshness of it was quite a strain at first, but the strength of commitment and humour of the others under command helped greatly. So here at last was the clean and honest structure for which I had been looking for so long. I had joined the monastery looking for a purifying discipline and I certainly found it. Gradually I began to like it. The pseudo-sophistication of adolescence fell away and I was greatly simplified. The mechanism of punctuality, of being summoned by bells, of fulfilling certain tasks by a certain time, became a pleasure. I realized that I could live any disciplined life, however hard: that discipline was easy.

Had we just had the rigid structure, we would soon have tired of it: it was monotonous and sometimes humiliating. In fact Father Alban's novitiate was very positive: he taught us a love of prayer and the desire to live a life wrapped up in God. I heard for the first time consciously of the love of God, about the ever-presence of God and the way every thought could be a means to forget oneself and one's fears and make one aware of him. To an outsider all that may seem very abstract and pointless, but to me the depth of commitment, a common experience we all shared, is one of the most valuable and meaningful of my whole life. Prayer is not just a state of suspended animation, like a cow asleep on its feet, nor a form of athletic trick by which one achieves in some way a stretching of the person: what is so hard for an outsider to understand, so hard for someone who lives for his activities to believe in, is that prayer is positive at all. Yet it is like a drug: it brings you to know a new world; not a drug like LSD which kills experience and finally man himself, but like love for a young wife or like writing poetry. Prayer gives you experience. Thus it was that in this year 1946 I began reading the simple manuals of prayer: Grou, Boylan and Merton, authors who treated of method and technique, like those little red military drill books that drill sergeants carried around. We quickly passed on to the masters: Teresa of Avila, John of the Cross and – for me the most satisfying of all – the English Mystics. My Odyssey was made in an English ship. The Downside of the time was no sentimental place; its prayer too was a form of intellectual exercise, not an emotional experience. Part of the Downside folklore runs as follows:

> *Monk:* Father Abbot, I thought I really ought to inform you: I am having visions.

> *Abbot:* Oh no, no, Father; we definitely don't have visions at Downside.

For a young man of eighteen, the prayerful community was full of hope and learning. To me it was all new; and I found that most of the community I had known so long and scrutinized without comprehension was involved in it. There were high seas to cross and I went about it with zest. Nobody who has been through that discipline and had that inspiration will ever forget it.

Strangely, this perfectionist society had been very largely developed by a man who for ten years remained a ghost in our midst. When at last I met him, he turned out to be the Professor of Medieval History at Cambridge. At Downside even the skeletons in the cupboard turn out to be intellectuals. The name, Dom David Knowles, the king over the water Cam, was never mentioned in the novitiate; yet Father Alban had been his right-hand man, and the new Abbot, Dom Christopher Butler, his close associate during the 'Usque Movement' of the 1930s. This movement had looked to bring about a monasticism really apart from the world: a monastery leading a truly simple prayer life and having time for truly scholarly work; or, on the negative side, no parishes, no public school. Father Alban taught the desirability of such a wonderful life and tried to make us regret the necessity of an active life. Two of my contemporaries left and joined the Cistercians; both became novice masters in their turn, and I too paddled in Cistercian waters, visiting Caldey Island where Father Alban himself had gone when the Usque Movement lost momentum in the 1930s. I did not read the actual words of Dom David until in 1980 *Dom David Knowles, A Memoir* by Dom

Adrian Morey, came to hand. In the 'Project for a Contemplative Foundation, 1933', under 'Poverty', come these suave sentences: 'We would aim at simplicity in everything. Individual poverty would be as extreme as possible; community possession not such as to give the impression of a "comfortable" life.' I find myself almost speechless in face of this, because these words about poverty show me the limits of my courage and perhaps that of my whole generation. I, for one, have been dishonest about poverty all my monastic life, unable, for all my love of discipline, to bring myself to fulfil my aspiration and my vow. I entered the monastery seeking honesty and duty and they were shown to me; but somehow as with most studies that required concentration and real spirituality, I failed to go on seeking.

Downside was not just a seven-storey spiritual mountain. It had that style and culture which I met first when I was taught by Arbuthnott. After that first year in the novitiate, Fr Illtyd Trethowan took me in hand and fed me books. Starting with Belloc's *The Path to Rome*, I read 200 books in two years. My interests became wide and rather superficial: heraldry and genealogy (my father's interests), painting, sculpture, architecture and, most of all, literature. Father Illtyd built for me a new structure side by side with the Knowles spiritual edifice. On the basis of my really great incompetence, he developed my critical awareness and a love of 'style'. Those years as a Junior seem Arcadia now, a Glass Bead Game.

So the foundation and structure of the ship was built. It was a structure built to last, of English oak, and it keeps its shape still, though it is buried in sand and would need an archaeological operation to uncover it. It was a frame built of duty and vow, and it is surprising how little, at least theoretically, friendship came into it. 'You are happy as a monk?' people ask from time to time. To me, a meaningless question. I built my monastic vessel because it was worth while, of value, and would help me to sail away from my lubber selfishness and my self-content; it was a means to truth, not to happiness. The Downside construction was so strong that I was unaware that it excluded knowledge of, and friendship with, women; and that acquaintance with other young men was almost entirely excluded. On the other hand, for twenty-five years I had no problems with sex and even thoughts were excluded. Also, that race of giants, the family, was largely forgotten. The daily liturgy, the plainchant and ceremonies, the academic studies and, above all, the honour and glory of being a Gregorian, a Downside monk, was all. I raced through my simple vows, my solemn vows, my priestly ordination, almost without a thought. That underworld life, that real world I had met in family and school, had been left behind on the coast.

Cambridge in 1952 might have shaken the structure and altered my course, but it hardly made any difference. I studied too hard, enjoyed myself too little and was awarded the bad degree I deserved. I was a typical student of those earnest post-war days; I would have liked to act, to take part in literary societies, but I did not have the spirit of independence required and I passed them by. But the quality of the English Literature teaching I received was superb. I sat at the feet of Dr F. R. Leavis and Dorothea Krook. I learnt not just to know about something but to look beyond and develop taste and judgement. Literary criticism, which so easily can appear a matter of sorting dry peas, is really an exercise in moral judgement, and exacting, both as an intellectual exercise and as a moral one. I discovered that in Cambridge few arts students had any religion, because their studies developed a strong independence of moral judgement and a flexibility and originality which do not fit in well with packaged theology. This experience of being one's own pilot, of there being different codes and charts, could and perhaps should have changed my horizons, but it did not. My monastic training was quite enough to allow for a little individualism or moral eccentricity; in fact eccentricity was in a way encouraged; but a radical change of course was unthinkable. It was a commonplace idea that one came down from Cambridge to find real education and originality at Downside.

But when I came down from Cambridge it was not to Downside. I went willingly enough to Worth, the daughter house of Downside, and since 1956 I have hardly ever returned to Alma Mater; in fact the monks there no longer seem my fellows, but another ship's company. There remains of course a strong nostalgia for the community I chose and which chose me, a tremendous gratitude for the vision and the grandeur of the place. But leaving it was like leaving the family: little communication took place, few letters passed, and friendship, such as it was, went into cold storage. So, strange as it may seem, the monastery of my profession, the church of my ordination, is now in no way my home.

At first, being at a dependent daughter house seemed much the same as being at Downside: the same thousand-year-old plainchant and prayers, the same eccentricities and manners. But I began to feel the boy-in-the-barrel experience again. Worth just did not have the leadership and momentum of Downside. There was not the same intellectualism, nor the same strong commitment to prayer and liturgy. One reason for this was that there was no novitiate there in those days, no young enthusiastic Juniors, nor a secondary school. Worth was, is and probably always will be a very happy place. It was then rich in the way my squire uncle's house in Cornwall had been wealthy: ponies, lawns and laughter. It was quite a new experience for me and the bark began to get barnacled with emotion. The strong structure built at Downside began to acquire a softness which my stony sisters would have hooted at. I competed with what I thought was a problem by working too hard at correcting the books of ten-year-olds and teaching myself and them the 'metaphysics' of English grammar. I finished my first year at Worth fairly seriously ill from overwork.

What might easily have developed into cynicism and utter loneliness was quickly overcome by the transformation of Worth under Abbot Victor Farwell. In 1957 Downside gave the house independence so that it could develop its own novitiate and its own secondary school. The process required great energy and the readiness to forget the past and look not too far into the future. Worth was not at first a very creative place. We followed the models of other Benedictine houses; I quickly took up the role of housemaster and later, as the Sixth Form developed, Head of English. Gradually this new structure developed and a new family emerged; we had little time to be introspective, but every inducement to build up a caricature and to live superficially. With so much to do, routine became very important. There were few concessions to the housemaster: Divine Office each day the same as everybody else, a teaching timetable and games almost the same as other teachers. Ten years went by almost unnoticed while I and my fellows toiled under a good headmaster at making a new school and keeping it in good order. Innovations began to be made; the school was not to be the ecclesiastical or priestly preserve my own schools had been. Laymen, non-Catholics and women were brought in to make it a 'multi-racial society'. Gradually around the dormitory and classroom there built up that network of loyalty and responsibilities, that group of friends and fellow workers, that seem normal to an English Benedictine house. Year by year and bit by bit history made itself, and tradition and character grew. I became immersed in it and so thoroughly that other structures outside Worth – the diocese, the family, other schools, other monasteries – lost importance. For six months at a time I would not leave the grounds, except once to Crawley (hardly Babylon) to buy clothes. In the early years I enjoyed the petty rivalries between house and house; I found a relish in the small duties of authority: fire officer, classroom cleaning and hounding smokers. But gradually I lost interest in those small mechanisms of housemaster's work, and the great values of teaching literature to sensitive people became paramount. I built up quite a large library in my panelled study, found ways of going to the theatre and of listening to the Third Programme *ad nauseam*; and I cast myself in the role of the intellectual. It was the old question of style again, style perhaps now against all other values.

Something had changed in those years during the build-up of Worth: I had not lost my faith, nor my innocence, but I had begun to lose interest in monasticism. The question implicit in my very entry into the monastery began to be asked again, and perhaps clearly for the first time. Was this whole structure of prayer and intellectualism, with its spice of style thrown in, just a way of avoiding my real world, the world beyond the green baize door? 'Style', by which I mean a love of beautiful things and working with panache, began as the years flicked by to be the only value. In the 1970s, after twenty-five years of being a monk, it nearly became a permanent alternative. Had that proved to be the outcome, it would have been outside the monastery.

Two things happened in the early 1970s which brought up the whole question of my real values and commitment, whether I could in honesty accept any longer the structure I had built. The first was Worth's decision to take part in some way in the Third World; the other was my making friends with women. The venture into Peru was one of Abbot Farwell's typically courageous innovations. He had the vision to see the need to 'come to terms with' the poor, to 'participate' in the problem of poverty. I was a supporter of the project after some initial doubts about the remoteness of the country and the difference of language. Three of us formed a committee to 'support' the four monks who would go out to the Apurimac jungle; very soon the committee consisted of one monk only, but I had the assistance of a keen secretary and we formed a central committee consisting chiefly of women, real pillars of the community. With these we founded the Friends of Peru, a body of about 2000 people who have with great loyalty and generosity supported the project for some ten years. It was an achievement I was and am proud of, though my own permanent contribution was the none-too-accurate name. Amid this activity, it was not possible to form committees and give lectures without driving here and there and spending a lot of time outside the monastery. I was excited at first by the wider horizons and the feeling that I was doing something for poor people, while

I lunched with the rich. Gradually the mixture of a well-organized monastic life, housemastering in a public school, teaching style and literature and now money-raising for the poor began to lead me into very rough spots. I began to get dissatisfied with my fellow monks, who were in fact very concerned and hardworking men, and to see them as caricatures and unfriendly shadows.

For a man who is not a monk, friendship with women is such an obvious necessity and pleasure that discovering a celibate who has had no female friends for twenty-five years is a joke if not a scandal. What harm are women, our sisters, likely to do? Does it really help to avoid their natural piety and sensitivity, which men so often lack? The fears are, of course, that such friendships will lead more and more to 'sexual involvement' and commitment to an individual as against spiritual involvement and commitmen. to the community. Gradually I took steps down this path, and of course I was amazed at discovering the humanity and richness I had never met before; also the sexual attraction whi:h I had been led to believe to be a hungry whirlpool was no great problem. The women I met and came to love must have been well disciplined and good people. Limits were set and new seas opened to me. Any non-monk would think that sailing those waters is necessary to the voyage, if not the object of the whole tour. But I was just at sea and discovering. I could shift the charts and sail one way on Thursday and Friday; but once out of the pond-like harbour of Worth, I would sail elsewhere. In fact this extraordinary interlude of some three or four years has, I believe, done me nothing but good. Two women friends have taught me that I could be loved, not least by my own brethren and family. They taught me that really to live the caricature of the fierce schoolmaster, the hated Chalky, was not necessary, and that the pleasure I took in being disliked or feared was very silly. It will take a lifetime to cure me of being a malcontent, but the new course started in those years. The spiritual-intellectual vessel with all its style and value began to feel as though it sailed on a painted ocean; the real world of personal relationships, with all their difficulties and pleasures, came back on the flood, in much the same way as the Pentecostal or Charismatic Renewal Movement swept back into the Church after the Second Vatican Council. During all this time I kept my discipline of prayer and community life and followed the dull round of housemastering, but still took joy in teaching Shakespeare. But muddle I had not experienced since

I left school years before shook my timbers, upset my brethren and even disturbed the family.

What happened was that for the second time in my monastic life I underwent a complete change. It was agreed in December 1974 that, after twenty years at Worth and ten at Downside, I should go to Peru. I, who for so long had preached the needs of the Third World, could hardly say, whatever the state of my love life, that I did not want to go. Whether the Abbot or the Headmaster (whom I had not kept in ignorance of my wandering course) thought a new start was what I needed, I do not know, but certainly there was need for change in our Peruvian jungle monastery and at forty-five I was not too old to take part. 'Did I want to go?' That is not a question one should ask me; the discipline I had learnt as a young man under a good colonel had not weakened; and in fact it was not difficult in July 1975 to leave my monastic uniform behind, disperse my library, hand over my house to a layman and leave my second family behind. In a way I was used to that sort of thing. But of course, to leave my first close friends, to leave my brethren whom I was just getting to appreciate and all the comfort of twenty years' routine, was not pleasant. But arriving off the plane at Lima airport, I was met by friends and it all appeared a soft landing.

During the late 1960s and early 1970s, of the great numbers of priests who came down from the States or over from Europe to South America, sometimes as many as half in one year gave up their priesthood and got married, often to their teachers. Emotionally, if you have been happy at home, the cultural shock is tremendous. I, for one, went through emotional upsets and muddle. The first shock was to find that it was a lie that one could learn Spanish, an easy language, in three months; the normal time to fluency is three *years*. The second shock was to find that effectively all communication with England was cut off. So there were no friends, and it takes six years to make friends in such a country. Thirdly, in times like that, when there are storms, one begins to disbelieve the charts and disbelieve the whole monastic interpretation of life. It was as well for me that I was in an emotional vacuum at the time; the extent of the problems and the emptiness of life helped me to grit my teeth and to take it. I was a novice again at the age of forty-five; hardships and humiliations were part of life. Gradually I rowed out of the storm, as better men than I had done before. As we set up our new community in Lima, itself an urban jungle, the small community had for its leader Fr Edward Cruise, an extremely tough personality, older than I and one who suffered much worse than I in Peru. He organized what is now known as a small sharing community; he helped greatly. We built the normal Benedictine bark: regular Office, common meals, quite a lot of silence; and recently that indispensable element in monastic life, the novitiate, has been set up. Another new structure and another bulwark against the waves of the real world outside, you might think. But that is not so; for me at least, something quite new has happened.

What happened, then? Did my new friendships with women and a few months in a caring community cure the sourness in my stomach and settle the urge to rebellion? The cold look, the apparent cynicism, the great reliance on 'style' are still there; also the restlessness and muddle. The discipline is firm: I hold it nothing to leave home, to avoid marrying, to give up smoking or drinking; these are all something any man can do. What is happening is that I am gradually stepping back into the real world again, with all its struggle between people, and I realize that what I have avoided for so long, the purpose for which I built the craft in the first place, has a name and is something many of us stylish intellectual people hate so much. It is POVERTY.

It is not a Third World I step into willingly. Too many names buzz through my head: Shakespeare, Arbuthnott, Knowles, Downside, Worth, Dominic, those two special women friends. But bit by bit, I am going to step into this world and leave the rest behind. If necessary, I may have to leave a wreck on the shore, perhaps with a few survivors. I wonder whether I can ever return to those shells, those so English structures, I left behind those years ago? I have taken off my sixteenth-century monastic costume because I cannot meet poor men, ordinary men in a real world, dressed like a sober character in *Star Wars*; ordinary Christians deserve to be treated with greater courtesy and consideration. I find more and more that the people I came to help know more about humility in face of adversity, about courage and self-discipline amid real personal difficulty, than I have learnt in thirty years of hiding behind a 'foxy' mask (my school nickname). The theology I knew has been overturned and a new honesty has to look again at the basic Christian truths. Who could worry about whether Christ is present in the Mass by way of transubstantiation or in some other form, when Christian parishioners are shot in the streets by the Civil Guards? This is not the time to finger the theological frets, nor the time to dawdle amid flying buttresses, nor the time to waste polishing up the intellectual fingernails of the public-school rich. A monastic life that does not have the compassion to share with the poor man, the ordinary man, with Jesus of Nazareth, is a medieval intellectual sham. I know that our Benedictine prayer must be remade out of a common experience of poverty, out of a new need for music and joy amid hunger. In the end the poor men, the Nazarenes, will do it themselves without much help from us, the rich; but it is a great honour to get near to Christ, to see him at his wood, to watch him sweat and to hear the hammer on the nails.

So you love being in Peru? No; it's awful.

Editor's note: Within a month of writing his Odyssey, Father Fabian died suddenly while on leave at Worth Abbey. We should like to reproduce here the address given by his Abbot, Fr Victor Farwell, at Father Fabian's funeral.

A few years ago I asked a small group of monks and nuns of the English Benedictine Congregation to write a book about their experience of monastic life which might be of interest to the lay reader. The book has been written and will, I hope, shortly be published. One of the contributors was Father Fabian and he entitled his chapter 'Monastic Malcontent'. I should like to quote from his opening paragraph: 'My monastic Odyssey is not quite the edifying tale of the other contributors to this book. Their happiness shines through like members of a ship's company under a good captain. I was, even as a boy, the sort of person who hid in a barrel and ate green apples; as a man, the sort of official who quickly became first mate and thought of mutiny. It has been my fate to stumble constantly into the wrong camp; my life has been a continuous political campaign, full of chaos and muddle . . . My Odyssey finds me still at sea and in far waters off the coast of Peru; still sailing, still lost . . . Mine has been a very difficult life for other people.'

Those who knew Father Fabian only slightly should not misunderstand these words; we, his brethren, recognize them as typically Fabianic: that is, deliberately different, unorthodox and nonconformist. Father Fabian was certainly an unusual monk; the Rule of St Benedict caters for all sorts, but you don't often meet a Fabs, as he was affectionately known, in the cloister. In the 1950s he would have been called an Angry Young Man; yes, he was angry, dissatisfied, all his life, but he was angry with the right things: with half-truths, with pious clichés, with unproven assumptions; above all, he was dissatisfied with himself and with what he regarded as his failures to reach the enormously high standards that he set himself as a monk and as a Christian. His wasn't the dissatisfaction of a man who wants to opt out, but of a man who wants to opt in, to go the whole hog. In this he was a Christlike figure; like Jesus, he was utterly committed but wanted to go further and deeper than was conventional. If he was full of discontent, it was a divine discontent.

St Benedict says that a monk's primary task is to seek God. For some of us this is a relatively uncomplicated task, but not for Father Fabian; his mind was never still and his capacity for trying new approaches was very marked. As a housemaster he was renowned for running Chapman House on strictly unorthodox lines; the word 'Fabianic' became an expression for anything bizarre, novel or unexpected. One result of this was that, as housemaster, he had a very fruitful apostolate with unconventional intelligent boys, with difficult or angular boys; he could understand their dissatisfactions, their restlessness, their quest for an ideal. Many people in trouble turned to Father Fabian, because instinctively they knew he would understand. He was able, like St Paul, to make himself all things to all men. I think he resembled St Paul in other ways too; he could be intolerant and unreasonable; he could be angry; but he was capable of great affection, sensitivity, gentleness and compassion. St Paul fought with wild beasts at Ephesus; Fabian fought with the half-wild dogs of Lima. I like to think that these Peruvian mongrels were projections of his subconscious self; Fabian was determined to master, dominate and tame them as he was determined to master himself. Like St Paul, he drove himself hard; both Paul and Fabian were workaholics, never at rest, always on the move, determined and ruthless in pursuit of spiritual goals.

When Father Fabian was a housemaster, it used to be said that he enjoyed—in every sense—a love-hate relationship with those around him. He enjoyed war because he was at war with himself. Then he went to Peru and there—so it seems to me—he came to terms with himself and achieved a serenity that he had not previously known. 'I am gradually stepping back', he wrote, 'into the real world...into a monastic life that has the compassion to share with the poor man, the ordinary man, with Jesus of Nazareth... It is a great honour to get near to Christ, to see him at his wood, to watch him sweat and to hear the hammer on the nails.' He wrote those words a few weeks before his death; at that time, as we have seen, he thought of himself as 'still at sea, still sailing, still lost'. Happily, on this last point he was quite wrong; his sudden death last Sunday—the day of

Christ's resurrection—indicated that, as far as God was concerned, Fabian had reached the shore.

But I should be failing him if I concentrated too much on the memory of his goodness and all the good it was given him to do, to the extent of forgetting that he may still need the help of our prayers. I know he would expect all those whom he loved, admired and respected to pray for the repose of his soul, just as he would pray for theirs.

May he rest in peace.

Cast Your Bread on the Waters

DOM DOMINIC GAISFORD

I suppose the first thing I want to say is that I have (so far!) enjoyed being a monk. Perhaps I am not only fortunate in this, but unusual? I can't recollect struggles of any searing kind between me and my monastic vocation, not either/or struggles. I always seem to be struggling to become myself within my vocation – yes, but not against it. This is not to say that I haven't often thought and felt how satisfying it would be to be married and have a family or to have the freedom of the laity, but these are not radical struggles. I put them in the same category as those facing a happily married man who may from time to time wish he were married to someone else with a different home and family and job. In short, such dissatisfactions with myself in the monastery are in essence escapist, not root-doubts about whether I am a round peg in a square hole. I sometimes reflect that I would probably feel more tied and circumscribed in being married to one woman and family, my horizons would be more limited, my friends less numerous and varied than I experience and enjoy as a monk. I like and enjoy the friendship and vagaries of my brethren too; they mean an enormous amount to me, as well as the wide range of friends outside the enclosure which enriches me, and which I owe to my monastic vocation.

Does this sound a trifle complacent or euphoric? I hope not, because what attracts me to the monastic life now is the constant demands it makes on me: to love others more, to love God, to love myself as I am. My frustrations, loneliness, struggles come from an ever-growing awareness of my failures in these three respects.

But to return to my first point: enjoyment, or rather, joy. To be a Christian must bring joy or else we are the most miserable of men. Yes, frustrations and suffering, of course; but to follow Christ, to be one with Christ, to be loved by Christ must be an abiding deep fount of joy, whatever the pain that may accompany us on our pilgrimage with Christ back to his Father.

So a monastery should be a home, where there is joy, and I do find joy in mine. Our homes, whether lay or monastic, should be joyful places, and if they are not we must all fall to prayer together to find out how and why we are blocking the peace of Christ coming into us.

I was born in 1928 at Old Delhi in India, in the autumn of the British raj: my father and grandfather lived and worked in the princely States, and I took it for granted that I would do the same. But when I was about fifteen my father told me that soon there wouldn't be a raj. Perhaps some would say that joining the English Benedictines was the next best thing one could do?

Certainly India made a deep impression on me, possibly at root a romantic one. My father was an ardent practitioner of yoga— rather *outré* for an Englishman of that time—and I remember being asked when I was twelve if I was the son of the Gaisford fellow who stood on his head every morning for half an hour before breakfast, which is in fact what he did, but not for half an hour. He had an enormous respect for the mystical traditions of India, though I don't remember him actually talking about prayer. The vast horizons and antiquity of India also predisposed me to regard it as normal and natural that God should be an integral part of my life, and to see that the most striking and obvious fact about everything is its inherent mysteriousness.

The family commuted between India and 'home' until war broke out, when my father took us (my mother, my sister and two brothers and myself) out to India in July 1940 to be with him. I returned to England towards the end of the war to continue my schooling at Downside. The voyages both ways had moments of excitement: on the way out I was aged eleven and a half and I found it simply exciting when our ship was bombed at sea; three years later and three years older I discovered that I was frightened when we were chased by submarines.

My early life in India was by modern standards an extremely bad training and one of its annoying by-products is that I am pretty useless at anything practical. We lived in grand residences, stayed in palaces with maharajahs, travelled by special train and in general lived like royalty, whom my father was in fact representing. I remember a bathe in the sea he once took in a State in South India. On arrival at the beach he found that an enormous tent (with chairs and a fresh-water bath in it) had been put up on the sand. When he had changed in the tent a red carpet had been rolled from it down to the sea. My father walked down it to the strains of 'Rule Britannia' played by a military band. On entering the sea he was knocked over by a wave which dislocated his shoulder and forced him to make a quick and humiliating return up the red carpet. The band promptly played 'God Save the King', so he had to stand to attention in his bathing costume, trying to look dignified.

My last eighteen months in India were spent at an Indian boarding school in Rajkot, the birthplace of Mahatma Gandhi. The school was run on English public school lines and was a remarkably good one. The very few English boys there wore Indian clothes on Sundays and I still relish the opening words of its prospectus: 'A school for the sons of English gentlemen and Indian princes' (in that order).

I spent three years at school at Downside and during my last couple of terms I decided to apply to join the novitiate. What were my reasons?

I had had no physical home during my childhood and boyhood, being always on the move between England and India and also within India, so the stability of Benedictine life appealed to me. During my holidays in England when my parents were in India I shuttled between kind aunts and friends, so I had no home and led a rather unexciting life. Downside became my home and was more fun than the holidays. Once I accepted the fact that India held no future for me, the kind of life Downside offered seemed to me to be more fulfilling than anything I knew or could think of. In the mid-1940s and as the war ended, I wanted something committed and absorbing. I thought that Downside was where I would find happiness. So my reasons for joining were probably half escapist and half (romantically) positive. They were not very profound, nor am I particularly proud of them now.

I was clothed in September 1948, made my solemn profession in 1952 and was ordained priest in 1954. I went to Cambridge in 1955, where I read History. It was while I was at Cambridge that an event took place which changed my life, namely the grant of independence by Downside Abbey to Worth Priory (now Worth Abbey) in Sussex.

Worth had been founded in 1933 as a dependent house of Downside. By 1957 it was sufficiently established for Downside to follow the Benedictine custom of giving a dependent house its independence and full autonomy. In the spring of 1957, Abbot (now Bishop) Christopher Butler asked for volunteers to go to Worth to become members of the new independent monastery.

I wrote to the Abbot from Cambridge saying I had no wish to leave Downside and so would not volunteer for Worth. I then changed my mind for reasons that few would call spiritual. Fr Fabian Glencross (now in our mission in Peru) and I were on a bike ride in the Fens and we were discussing the new plans for Worth. Father Fabian told me he had volunteered, and that information sparked off my competitive spirit. I wrote that night to Abbot Butler, offering my services to Worth, and received a typically laconic postcard in reply: 'Thank you for your two letters, especially the last one. Yours affectionately, B. C. B.' And so I found myself at Worth in September 1957 as a founder member of the new independent community of nineteen monks under Fr Victor Farwell. I have never regretted my decision and am deeply grateful to Abbot Butler for selecting me.

I finished Cambridge in June 1958. I was sad to leave, for it also emphasized that I was finished with the Downside part of my life. I had become a reluctant member of the new community at Worth, for all my interests, roots and affections were centred on Downside and the Mendips. My last year at Cambridge, with Downside monks, allowed me to pretend that nothing had really changed in my life. It was in this nostalgic spirit that Father Philip Jebb (now headmaster at Downside School) and I decided to bicycle at the end of the term, as my leaving gesture, from Cambridge to Downside. There was no question of my biking to Worth! We spent a night at Oxford and did it in two days. I had loved long bike rides on Month Days and in August, and this ride was in the tradition of the Downside I loved. My memory is that those two days biking across England were halcyon sunshine.

It was Prize Day weekend at Downside when we arrived. Father Wilfrid Passmore (then headmaster and later Abbot of Downside) met me in the church, by sheer chance, and he took me aside by Cardinal Gasquet's tomb and hinted in his inimitable way that a big important job awaited me at Worth. Though he didn't actually say I was to be headmaster of the new Upper School we were about to open, I knew that this was what he meant. So when Father Victor, the Prior of Worth, asked me a few days later to become headmaster, it wasn't really a surprise.

How did I feel at the prospect? Looking back, I realize that I was pretty callow and superficial—I was aged thirty—and yet my reactions then were what they are now to any job or work I'm asked to do. I don't think I've changed all that much! One half of me was excited, I felt I was the obvious person for the job, that I would somehow make the best school in England; the other half was deeply alarmed that I should be found out to be the rather mediocre and shallow person that I am, masquerading under pseudo-winning colours. I'm not sure that God came into the picture very much in any deep, real way – I felt it was all up to me. I have a competitive streak in me and I like to compete with God to be No. 1 in my life.

I don't think I ever really doubted that the new school would be a success, which is not the same as saying there weren't moments of great anxiety and moments of doubt; and the reason for this unshakeable confidence, I can now see in retrospect, was simple. Father Victor always gave me his full support, confidence and affectionate encouragement, whatever his private doubts and hesitations may have been. It is a satisfying and great experience to be believed in and this I had in full measure from him. And I felt the same from the community. I never felt anyone had his knife in me and I knew I could rely completely on the support of the monks. I'm not implying there was no criticism or that I didn't feel critical of some monks over the way they did (or didn't do) things, but at heart we were at one. I have become more aware of how God acts in my life through this experience of support and trust from the community. If I am believed in and trusted I can do almost anything. So I've come to realize how deeply dependent I am on people and through this I am coming to realize my dependence on God as even deeper; left to myself I can do nothing.

I also realize now, despite being very busy then, how little I actually did to make the school grow and succeed (more about 'success' later). It was other monks who carried the heat and burden of the day, by which I mean not only heavy timetables, but giving the boys friendship and time and concern, so that the school became more and more human as the years went by. This taught me my dependence on others, and my limitations, the hard way. I found I was not a man for all seasons and for all people, but limited. This was an extremely valuable discipline which saved me from arrogance and deep conceit as the school progressed and became established. I made it a rule to try to give others credit and praise or to pass it on to them. I often broke my own rule and hugged things for myself, but I did try. So I learned tolerance, in the sense of knowing that whatever is good in me and in others comes not from us but from God – it is a gift – and I learned how to marvel at the goodness, selflessness, initiative and warmth of others. The glory of God is a living man. I certainly became more aware of this truth, though I was at the same time envious of the people who enjoyed gifts and gave them to others in ways and degrees I couldn't emulate.

I learned the hard way about the unpredictable mysteriousness of people and that all problems are to do with people, not systems. I once gave a master legal notice because he wasn't as stimulating as I hoped; I wanted his department to be good and prestigious, a selling point for the school. He and his wife were very popular with the staff, who rose in wrath against me, presented me with petitions and saw the Abbot. I had put my ambitions for the school, my plans, before the human needs of a couple. So I compromised and gave him a year and a term's notice. It was an extremely painful experience to be disliked and mistrusted by virtually the whole staff, but it was salutary for me. I suppose I was given an insight into the patience of God, who has to wait and wait for us to repent and improve, has to be content with the second or third best in us. I had many similar experiences with boys whom I judged to be a bad influence and disrupting the school: that is, upsetting my plans and ambitions for the school and its image. I was too prone in my early years to use the knife of excision for what I thought then were the highest motives. I didn't fully understand or study chapters 27 and 28 in the Rule of St Benedict about the solicitude an abbot ought to have, until my last few years.

I was very much influenced in my earlier years as headmaster by my novitiate training: to be aloof from people, to be impartial to everyone and so close to no one, to be self-consciously a monk all the time. This had a very valuable side to it in terms of self-discipline and to some extent forced me to rely on God to shoulder the burdens, but I wonder now if the boys benefited from it. It was the friendship and affection of a few families – in particular, the wives – that slowly showed me they liked me for myself and not because I was headmaster. This was a warming and maturing experience and I wish it had happened sooner. It helped me to relax and grow in confidence and with it came the close friendship of some boys in the school. It is vital that religion and God should have a human heart and face. It is only too easy for someone like me, as a headmaster with a demanding and time-consuming workload, to find that there is little time for human relationships, to let 'duty' rule the day. I'm sure this is a problem facing married men and women all the time: work can drown the person. It didn't drown me entirely because of the support I always got from the Abbot and community and some special families, but the experience of how work can make someone become not exactly superficial but very limited, as it did me, highlights a challenge facing us monks today.

Once during my time as headmaster and again when I retired I was fortunate enough to visit our small monastery in Peru. In 1969

Worth had established a small monastic mission in the Apurimac valley in the eastern slopes of the Andes. Abbot Victor Farwell was inspired to do this in response to the call of the Second Vatican Council and to pleas for help from some South American Benedictines whom he met in Rome. We at Worth felt that, whatever our manpower problems might be, we should do what we could to found a pastoral monastery in the Third World, and we happened by chance to have had an invitation to come to Peru. On the two occasions when I visited it, I stayed a month each time.

There is a huge culture shock to absorb once you leave 'First World' Lima and move into 'Third World' Lima and the Andes. On my first visit I drove over the Andes to our mission: an awesome drive, in which we went over four passes of 14,000 feet each. On arrival in the valley, I remember being taken in a large dug-out canoe down the Apurimac valley by a local official who was trying to explain to me the political philosophy of the then Peruvian government. We were going through some rapids and he emphasized his points by slapping the sides of the canoe so heavily that it tilted over and took in some of the river: '*Capitalismo* – bad (slap); *comunismo* – bad (slap); *cooperativismo* – good' (two slaps). On my second visit in 1977, the Abbot and I arrived in the small hours during a military coup. At first I thought it exciting, in a Gilbert and Sullivan way, as our taxi drove through a deserted Lima. Each of us, including the driver, had to have one hand hanging out of the window holding a white handkerchief. We were frequently stopped by military patrols. My view changed when near our monastery we saw a family being shoved into an armoured car and as we turned the corner we heard shots. I regret to say that none of us went to investigate. The violence which sometimes erupts there is born of the fear of grinding poverty, but my overall impression was that of the Peruvians' gentleness and courtesy, their hospitality and their ability to laugh where we would cry in despair. On my visit to one house, my host said to me, 'How nice of you to come, but when is Queen Elizabeth going to visit us?'

This is not the place to describe the venture, but I can say emphatically that the six Worth monks in Peru, now working in a poor area of Lima, have brought new life and vision to Worth itself, apart from the hope and pastoral compassion they are bringing to the people they serve out there.

Back at base, my life as headmaster was extremely busy and 'full of one damn thing after another', as the Abbot of Buckfast once described it. Just coping with the flow of events in itself yielded the kind of satisfaction I used to get as a junior monk after a marathon bike ride around Somerset on a Month Day, when we just got back in time for Vespers – made it! I was building up something, a new school, which was external to myself, not me, and yet it was an extension of me. It brought out the competitive spirit in me and I wanted success, though I hope in not too crude a sense. I never wanted to use boys as stepping-stones to my success, though I'm sure I did on occasion willy-nilly. The school had a great deal of success by the grace of God and by the skin of my lucky teeth, but the two areas in which I most of all wanted to succeed remained frustratingly closed to me, so that, in terms of my scale of priorities, these years were not fundamentally successful. I wanted the school to be a place where the boys found and kept their faith, so that they would keep it in later life and Christ would be as important to them as their A levels and careers. This just did not occur! The other area was personal: I wanted the boys to regard me as a priest and friend and not an authority figure. I think I wanted them pouring into me for advice as to a friend. This was tied up with my desire that boys, on leaving the school, should regard Worth not so much as a school but as their religious home. I don't think I had much success in this area either, though more than in the former. I'm sure the experience of failing to achieve what I wanted was essential to the rediscovery of a 'deeper' God in my life.

I think we have to be careful not to confuse the growth and success of a system or structure with personal growth and maturity. Or, to put it another way, I was always tempted to identify the success and growth of the school with myself. To some extent people in responsible jobs must do this in order to act responsibly, but the danger is that the function becomes the person. I remember being thrilled when our first block of study bedrooms was built, because I felt that this would make the Sixth Formers happy and then all would be well. Similarly the pleasure of getting increasing numbers of university entrances or Oxbridge awards made me feel the school was good and so I was good. I was delighted later on when I became a member of the Headmasters' Conference – delightful, charming, amusing, dedicated professionals who made me feel that Worth and I had arrived at the top of the greasy pole of successful and urbane schools. And yet the moment I got into the charmed HMC circle – which I enjoyed unashamedly – I knew instinctively that this wasn't what a 'school of the Lord's service' was about (to quote the Rule of St Benedict) and I found the taste of the fruit frothy. I kicked myself for enjoying aping the world of public schools – and went on enjoying it.

I think the same situation can arise in a monastic context: one can identify oneself with the monastic structure, with good liturgy, fine buildings, a strong tradition influencing one's behaviour, humour and way of life, attracting guests, novices and old boys to the place and gaining respect from the outside world. All these are good and necessary, but they can so mould the personality that a monk becomes simply an amalgam, as it were, of these structural qualities which make up a successful monk and monastery. But we must be more: we must be ourselves, fully human and filled with the desire to seek God and be involved with people.

I know that being a monk has made me what I am and given me, especially as headmaster, opportunities and challenges I would probably never otherwise have had, in meeting a whole host of people and being involved in their lives, which is tremendously enriching. Yet the witness we have to give should be something more than that of a model monk; grace should complete human nature and make it whole. Our intellects, emotions, affections, ambitions and needs have to be integrated and transformed by the grace of Christ mediated to us in the monastic way of living. This is an exhilarating challenge. We have to show that living the gospel as monks has made us full-blooded human beings. To be a Christian should transform everyone and make them really human, not less so.

Monasteries should be warm and open places where friendship and affection can be given without fear, where we seek the best in people without abrasive competition, where efficiency is tempered by solicitude, where all the complexities of sin in us are slowly healed by prayer and the sacraments, and where hope is found. It is not easy to integrate all the conflicting elements in us, ranging from sexuality via fruitful work and intellectual satisfaction to the search for God in himself and in others, but it can and must be done if we monks are to fulfil our vocation as prophets and witnesses to the Good News of Jesus Christ.

I think celibacy is a more difficult ideal to take in and a more demanding way of life to lead these days than when I was a novice. The absence of intimate sexual relationships has always been hard, but the modern emphases on personal fulfilment, on developing and exploring one's talents and endowments, on shying away from suffering and on avoiding frustrations, all tend to accentuate acutely the negative aspects of celibacy. Added to this, our increasing dependence on material and physical comforts and supports to living makes celibacy seem icier than in previous times.

Man is made for woman and woman for man. Each complements the other, as Genesis profoundly proclaims, and without such a complement I remain, at one level of my being, but partially fulfilled. Everyone needs and wants to give intimacy (which is not to be identified with the physical), and this is perhaps the heart of our sexuality. The sexual urge is God-given. It gives a dimension and force to everything we think and do, including our prayer. It is an urge to give myself as fully as I can. It is an integral part of companionship, of love and of living. As we mature, each of us develops our own sexuality, which gives a unique quality or force to our emotions, our affections, our bodily needs and language, our knowledge. In short, the way I love and receive love is special to me. It seems to me that our Western culture impoverishes our attitude to love and affection by identifying sexuality with physical and especially genital relationships neat, and by thinking in terms of 'How far can I go?' This kills trust, the heart of intimacy.

I am sure that God wants me – as he does every human being – to develop my powers of loving and my acceptance of love. So if I am to become truly alive, truly human, I need to love, to learn how to love and be loved, in relation both to God and to people. I can speak only for myself, but I am sure that for me loving must be rooted and grounded in my relationship to God; that without him my relationships would veer towards the fickle, the shallow and predominantly physical, and that this would cause me in the end as much, possibly more, frustration and sense of unfulfilment than celibacy can do.

The longer I live, the more I am aware of a reaching out for the intimacy of a man–woman relationship. I am not thinking simply or primarily of physical loving, but of the more wide-ranging trust or intimacy which is at the heart of companionship, which involves our affective sexuality, but which is distinct from physical intimacy.

And here I come to the paradox of why I am and remain committed to a celibate way of living. It is difficult to explain. While I am aware of an emptiness that calls out to be filled by a one-to-one relationship, I am also aware of another call from God to love him and other people in a different and celibate way.

It's as if I knew in my heart that God knows me better than I know myself, that if I married and worked at this great task of making a one-to-one relationship into a loving, lifelong trust, somehow I wouldn't be growing into the person God wants me to be; and so, though one part of me may wish otherwise, I wouldn't fulfil the potential that God has given me. I suppose that the need which I experience to relate intimately to one person, a wife, is at the same time God's call to me to go out beyond this in search of him, and in searching for him to try to reveal him to others.

There are, of course, definite limitations in the fulfilment of a one-to-one relationship; I wonder, for example, whether one woman would ever satisfy me for life (though I hardly ever wonder if I would satisfy one woman for life). Equally there are clear limitations in the one-to-many relationships which constitute the heart of community and monastic life. The chief of these is an inner loneliness which, while it is given meaning and a sense of purpose in prayer, remains at the same time an ache in the heart. But then marriage too has its aches of loneliness which should urge the partners on in the search for God, as they do for a monk.

I derive much pleasure and fulfilment from the wide range of friendships and affection I enjoy precisely because I am a monk. I suspect that monks can have more friends across the age groups and more friends of both sexes than most married men. I felt very complimented when my niece told me recently that I am 'tactile' in my affections. So these relationships are humanly satisfying and enriching. Celibacy has enabled me as a person who is a monk to be more available and open to people, to make many friends, and to give pastoral care and compassion that is in itself fulfilling.

But for me *the* reason for celibacy isn't to be found in the wide-ranging and affectionate friendships nor in the pastoral availability which monastic celibacy offers the monk and the people he tries to serve. In themselves they do not fill the loneliness of celibacy. So what is *the* reason for me?

I'm sure every human being is created and called to love some *one* person and to be loved back. At this point I come to the mystery of God's call to each person, to the mystery of why he has made me the sort of person I am. Though I do it fitfully, I believe God is calling me to love his Son, Jesus Christ, in a direct way, unmediated by the love that comes through the one-to-one relationship of marriage. Every Christian is called to love and follow Jesus Christ, but some seem to be asked to do it directly. I hardly dare to compare my love for Christ with St Paul's, but you can feel in his letters the vibrations of a man who was passionately in love with Jesus and who knew that God wanted him to love in this way, celibately.

So for me celibacy is God's way of leading me to love Jesus in a direct, unmediated way and then in that love to go out and love other people (some much more than others) in a genuinely human way, though of course without one kind of intimacy. And the joys of celibacy are friendship, living prayer and a fruitful ministry. For friendship is an expression of our need for intimacy and is a particular instance of our call to universal love. And the fruitful ministry comes from that inner urge, that inner restlessness in me, which makes me long to bring the Kingdom of God into the hearts of the people with whom I work and to whom I am committed. I can remember in the idealistic days of my early monastic life this longing, which seemed at times almost physical, to belong to Christ and to bring him to others. This may sound rather mystically impressive; it wasn't that impressive for it wasn't integrated into my daily living very well, but it does help me to understand that a call to a celibate way of living for Christ's Kingdom can be more imperative than the need I experience for the intimacy of a one-to-one relationship. Another paradox of which I am conscious is that the awareness of one need accentuates and increases the other and this must be good as it keeps me sensitive to the love of God and to the loveliness of human love.

As a monk I have committed myself to putting Christ as my first love, not for the sake of some spiritual orgasm, but to try to love as he loved by drawing people out of themselves and leading them to the Father. We do this by giving ourselves to others as best we can—in our work, through our affections, in our love. We use our sexuality, though we do not enjoy physical intimacy. Neither married love nor celibate love nor physical love can fully meet that innermost thrust of my being for total union, completeness. No other human being can of herself or himself fully quieten that restlessness in my heart which, as a Christian, I know and believe is satiated only when I am face to face with the sheer loveliness of God and romping around in the Communion of Saints. This of course happens at death, not before.

The seed of glory sown in man
will flower when we see your face.

So we live on a knife-edge: how to love God, always searching, yearning, aching for him as the centre point, the rock, the only fulfillment of our lives—and at the same time how to love men and women made in God's image and likeness. It is easier to do the one or the other: to take God and prayer and the monastic structure as a buttress and shield against the demands of loving people, or to throw oneself into work and relationships as an escape from the living God. But the glory of Christ is that he gives us the exhilarating power to do both, as he did. He worked to the

166

point of exhaustion, yet always prayed to his Father as the only person who could feed and sustain him; he enjoyed deep friendship with men and women which, while his sexuality was acknowledged as present, was in no way sexy; he spoke of the Kingdom and of hope but was never boring or pious. He was in every sense a full-blooded man in whom love cast out fears and inhibitions.

God's love is totally compassionate, never cools and is never disillusioned. And St Benedict's Rule, so enormously interested in people, is a rule of compassionate love: it assumes that the individual is sickly, wayward, lazy, possessive, stony of heart and thick in intellect. The pastoral care of the abbot and everyone else in the community is needed to heal and cure the sick brother, to help him to stumble along and then to run swiftly on the path of God's commandments.

The more I study the Rule the more I see it as a way of life for individuals-living-in-a-group. Individuals have to be compassionate in their love for the community; they have to coax, heal, nourish and jolly it along, to help it advance and not stay put. The individual must learn never to use the community as a means to his own ends, as an institution to be borne with while he lives his true life elsewhere. This is what Judas did and it was treachery. It is only compassion, the outgoing, gut-reaction love which unites and heals because it starts with people as they are, that can weld and re-create the divided, scattered and disparate into a living unity.

Commitment to a monastic community by life vows makes sense to me only if seen as a commitment to compassionate loving: to loving ourselves as we are (warts and all) and to loving the people we live with (warts and all). This kind of commitment may seem at times an act of irresponsible or even crucifying limitation; indeed it was so for Christ. Jesus was a Jew, not a Roman; he had twelve chosen friends, not an infinite number; he healed only a fraction of the sick in Israel; he never spoke to more than four or five thousand at a time. He was limited. God, who passionately loves all men, committed himself to loving in and through Jesus, a man of his times. This was an enormous act of self-limitation on his part. We have to do likewise: to commit ourselves to one person or one group, and in and through them learn compassion. Our powers of loving, and of loving compassionately, will paradoxically grow if we channel them, define and refine them. Promiscuity is not the seed-bed of love.

In 1970 we were wondering at Worth how we could be more open to the needs of others, of the laity. This mood of inquiry led us not only to go to Peru but also to start a new venture at Worth itself. So in 1971 the Abbot and community decided to try the experiment of inviting young laymen and women (especially in the eighteen-to-thirty age group) to come and live at Worth, in separate accommodation, and share as lay people in our rhythm of life: prayer, work, hospitality and relaxation. The invitation clearly met and still meets a real need among that age group. Under the inspiration of Fr Andrew Brenninkmeyer, some outbuildings were soon converted by the pioneer members into a welcoming home. A pattern established itself whereby six to ten young men and women live at Worth for twelve to eighteen months. They have jobs locally or at Worth, and out of their pooled salaries they have financed this conversion and provide for hospitality for weekend visitors: about 500 people a year now come to stay in the Lay Community. They join in the monastic prayer life but live their own life as a lay Christian community while they are at Worth. While the Lay Community seems to have helped and enriched those who come to it, it has certainly broadened and enriched my monastic life. It may provide a pattern for a new form of community living in the future in which monks, laymen and women can live, pray and work together and enjoy the experience.

In September 1977 I became prior, novice master and the monk responsible for the Lay Community. The difference between these last few years of my life and the seventeen I spent as headmaster now strikes me as a difference between 'doing' and 'being' though of course this is an over-simplification and a trifle arbitrary. The years since the change have been the most fruitful of all for me personally – I cannot judge how fruitful I have been for others – and I think I can now see why this is so.

While I was headmaster, my day had been so filled with appointments, interviews, paper work, attending school activities and teaching that not only had there been little time or occasion to be myself, but the nature and function of the office had tended to absorb me completely. When this came to an end, I felt extremely naked, as it were, and very bewildered. I had lost what had given me a large chunk of my identity and a range of activities which gave me a sense of being needed and of use to others. As novice master and in the Lay Community I have no comparable structures or pressures of people and paper work to give a pattern and order to my day. It dawned on me that what people wanted from me was not the function of my office but whatever it is that I have in me to offer. In a sense, I was on my own, not buttressed by an office which everyone clearly understands. And being on my own, I felt naked and pretty empty-handed.

For the first year, I can see (in retrospect), I floundered and missed the security of the school; in the second year I began to discover that I had a role and something to offer; in my third year I began to enjoy it in a new and invigorating way. The good fortune I have had is that these new jobs have helped me to integrate being a monk and being myself into a greater unity. I have come to realize that the very fact of being a monk (and a priest) enhances me. I have received much affection and support in the Lay Community because people seem to like me for what I am, and what I am has been largely created by my being a monk. I think it very important that one's faith, one's vocation, should make one more human, more oneself, because the glory of God is a living man, a man alive. And part of being truly alive is to acknowledge and accept one's failures and failings, one's sense of lack of fulfilment. All these have to be integrated, and this, I am now sure, can be done only by praying, by letting God into the secret of my innermost self and sharing it with him. So often other people think – and especially layfolk – that being a monk removes me from, or inoculates me against, failure and failings, and that my life is one happy success story. So it has been from one point of view, and I try to thank God for this, when I remember to, which isn't very often.

It seems to me that there are two levels or layers of *success*, and so two corresponding degrees of failure and non-fulfilment. The first level of success is that my job and responsibilities are carried out with efficiency. By and large, I achieved this in the school and laid a firm foundation on which others could build and are building splendidly. In the novitiate, I aim to create a reasonably mature and relaxed atmosphere by treating novices as adults who are joining me in the search for God. I am told that my way of running the novitiate is consistent in its inconsistencies and this pleases me in that it is at least a human characteristic and a good preparation for life in community. I flatter myself that the novices can find themselves and begin to find God in this atmosphere and that it is fairly successful as a training.

In the Lay Community I have set out to do the same thing: make it a relaxed and warm place where basic family humour and jokes are part of its spirit, so that people enjoy coming to it, as well as enjoying coming for prayer and the search for God. One fruit of this approach has been the emergence of a relationship between its members, and between the monks and the Lay Community, which I call sexuality without sex. By this I mean a relationship in which a man and a woman can grow in friendship which, while it springs from their complementary sexuality, isn't dominated by the somewhat grasping and aggressive sexual mores of today. If a lay or monastic community can help people to find a type of friendship which is the fruit of complementary sexuality rather than of sex it can make a real contribution to the healing of the loneliness which today afflicts so many people, married as well as single.

All this refers to one level of success. The second level is the more important and fulfilling one: namely, to practise what I preach. I am finding that good structures and good atmospheres are not sufficient, though they are vital foundations. Although I am busy, I have not been 'doing' much in terms of administration, or under pressure from scores of people and their activities, or planning people's futures. So these last few years have given me my first experience of 'being' since I was a novice, and this has been a painful but exhilarating experience: finding God again in prayer, finding out again how much I need him, how much I need human friendship and how much I depend on the community. It has shown me explicitly what I often sensed dimly when I was headmaster, namely a hollowness beneath the outward success and the undoubted satisfaction I got from a job reasonably well done. The hollowness was caused by the fact that my inner self or heart got somewhat dehydrated: it was never fully engaged or given to anyone. This was partly the result of my training, partly due to sheer pressure of time and events and partly because I didn't dare. I'm not meaning that I now wish I were married or am planning to have an affair with a lovely woman (though it might be fun!), but that I never gave myself fully as headmaster to anyone or anything or to God. This sense of partial fulfilment is, I suspect, at the root of many people's dissatisfaction with their jobs, their marriages, their communities: we discover that we have never given ourselves as fully as we imagined and so we blame everyone else and the circumstances.

I find it hard to give myself fully: I want to, but don't, and often wonder if I have anything much to give (to wallow in this is, of course, the sin of doubting the goodness and fidelity of God). I suspect that many people – monastic and lay – experience this same hollowness in their work-roles and jobs and perhaps don't always realize that they are experiencing it. They may also discover that complete heart-to-heart satisfaction and fulfilment in their marriages and communities seems to elude them, so they may turn either to new and harder work or to new marriages or new communities, or else they settle for a lower intensity and pitch of fulfilment in a saddened way. I suspect we all come face to face with moments of truth like this at different times in our lives.

What my time as novice master and in the Lay Community has illuminated for me is the awakened desire I have to give my real self and to be loved in return. I am experiencing the pain of new birth again; it is exciting and a little bewildering, but I thank God enormously for it. But I have also learned that I will not achieve what I long for either in a one-to-one relationship or in a community, so whether I were to stay here or leave to get married, the ache would continue. I am aware that in many deeply happy marriages there are also areas of loneliness or unfulfilment, so I am not romantic or naive enough to imagine that marriage is radically different from community life in respect of assuaging pangs of loneliness. Perhaps the chief cause of deep tensions in a married 'community' and a monastic one is the same? When a man (or woman) hopes and expects that all or most facets of his (or her) personality will be understood and filled by the other, and when he (or she) longs to be able to understand and fill the needs of the other, and when this does not seem to occur in the way we want, then the tensions of unfulfilled expectations are increasingly felt.

Is this the moment when we mature and can find God? Is this when our real search for the real God begins? For me, the answer is Yes. I have come to realize what I have known notionally for years, that no job, no rhythm of a work- and leisure-filled day, no human relationship however absorbing at first, can completely heal the tension in me. I know that only one person can do this, whom we call God. I am fortunate to live in a happy, integrated and affectionate community which is pervaded by a spirit of understanding and empathy, so I do not speak from a wounded experience – far from it.

Nor do I think, though I can't prove it, that I am taking refuge in prayer and God as an escape into wish-fulfilment. I'm sure that God is living love, that I am not using him merely as a God of the gaps in my life: on the contrary, I meet him in both the loneliness and the happiness, in the tension and the fulfilment of my life. I'm sure that I will always be restless until I rest in him; I'm sure that he is right here in the middle of me, that all my experiences are experiences of him, leading me right into him. He is not outside me but inside me, and he churns me up, so to speak, because he loves me and wants me and is restless himself until he gets me.

> When God at first made man,
> Having a glass of blessings standing by,
> Let us (said he) pour on him all we can:
> Let the world's riches, which dispersed lie,
>   Contract into a span.
>
> So strength first made a way;
> Then beauty flow'd, then wisdom, honour, pleasure:
> When almost all was out, God made a stay,
> Perceiving that, alone of all his treasure,
>   Rest in the bottom lay.
>
> For if I should (said he)
> Bestow this jewel also on my creature,
> He would adore my gifts instead of me,
> And rest in Nature, not the God of Nature:
>   So both should losers be.
>
> Yet let him keep the rest,
> But keep them with repining restlessness;
> Let him be rich and weary, that at least,
> If goodness lead him not, yet weariness
>   May toss him to my breast.
>
>   (George Herbert, 'The Pulley')

I am beginning to see, and maybe understand, that tensions arising from human relationships, and loneliness born of unfilled areas in me, are pretty essential to me in my search for God. I may even go further and, on a good day, say that without these things life would soon perhaps lose its savour. It is the paradox of the cross: I have to lose my life to find it. But of course on other days (and they seem to be the majority) I am always looking for immature short cuts and instant fulfilment. I pray I will go on maturing enough not to go too far down a short cut which will end in a cul-de-sac. This urgent ache for immediate lessening of tensions can coax any of us into affairs, workaholism, abandonment of prayer or just settling for a day-to-day pattern of life and relationships that is so taken up with small things that one becomes partially anaesthetized. And then, of course, one fights against any sort of change or jolt.

I know that when I was headmaster I was not fully alive to myself or to God, and when I look back on my regime my pride is chastened and my heart saddened at the opportunities lost thereby to boys, parents, staff and myself. This, I suspect, is an experience many parents have when they look back on the earlier years of their marriage. At the time I enjoyed chunks of my job and was pleased with what I was doing and achieving, but now I know better. That kind of success would not satisfy me now, because it was mainly at the first level of success of which I spoke earlier.

It seems to me that what monks and monasteries need, what many married people and families need, is a constant and continuing process of being made vulnerable, of being open to the adventure of human relationships all the time. This is not advocacy of wife-swapping or monastery-swapping – on the contrary – but advocacy of our need to be aware of our loneliness and sense of unfulfilment, so that we never settle down into a rut which anaesthetizes us. The sadness is when a monk or a married person evades and avoids tension or says, Well, that's life, and settles down to watch the box. Of course it is life, and watching the box is fair enough, so long as the fire hasn't gone out of us as a result.

From one point of view Christianity is the religion of failure, whereas we want and expect it to be a recipe for how to live our lives happily and contentedly. Christ's career was humanly a failure and deeply unsatisfying to him. No one really understood him or what he was about, not even his mother; he loved his friends far more than they loved him; he wanted and longed to help and love scores of people who just didn't want to know; his motives were always misunderstood and misjudged by friend and foe alike. Here are the ingredients of unrequited love on a massive scale that must have amounted to an almost intolerable experience for him of loneliness and failure. Our experience reflects Christ's: we too know unrequited love, and we live in a world of broken marriages and vows and unwanted life (which goes by the names of abortion and euthanasia), a world of fear and poverty.

So I ask, What were the ways that Christ's life was not a failure; in what constructive way does it speak to me? It seems to me that his love for his Father and for people increased almost proportionately to the measure of his lack of success in his 'career' and his human relationships. He didn't put up defences, he didn't settle for a cosy mediocrity, but he loved more than ever. He became more and more vulnerable in his loving and longing for people to come with him to the Father. At the same time his joy and contentment was to be with his friends and those he loved, even though he realized they wouldn't and couldn't meet all his needs or desires. Only his Father could do this for him.

I think my time with the novitiate and Lay Community is accentuating and integrating the sense of my need for human love and the love of God, of the contentment and the loneliness that ensue; and that in this experience I am becoming more alive.

One theme in particular has struck me in all the Odysseys in this book: it is that of growth, that a vocation is not a call from outside, but the perception and recognition by me of what I am, of what I am becoming. St Augustine said somewhere in a sermon to his people about the Eucharist – and I imagine him pointing to the altar and the bread and wine on it – 'See what you are, and become what you see'. This applies to ourselves. And this is growth: realizing more and more who I am and what I am, my needs and wants, my yearnings and longings, my areas of integrity and achievement, my areas of weakness, sin and inadequacy, my awareness of joy and sorrow – both of which are huge aches in differing ways.

Father Philip's 'Wonder is so Sudden a Gift' showed me growth through joy, and for him his many pains and anguishes (symbolized for me by the period he had of blinding headaches) seemed to be as joyous as his explicitly joyous moments of ecstasy. In Father David's 'Jigsaw' I found growth through pain, frustration and loneliness that tore at the roots of his being. In Father Alan's 'Love Bade me Welcome' growth has come through an interplay of certainty and uncertainty: in some passages in his story he says he found real peace and fulfilment (at Rome, for instance, and on finding charismatic prayer), and then in the next paragraph, so to speak, Father Alan is back in the sucking quagmire of doubts and uncertainty. Lots of deaths and resurrections, none of which is final, so he can't say, '*Consummatum est*'. This is so true to my experience. Sister Maria's 'Tapestry' seems to combine all these insights into growth, or vocation.

One of my overall impressions of these contributions is that I have not lived with such a variety of vivid and intense experiences. They are sparkling, heady wine, culled from many vineyards, while mine is a more ordinary pint of mild! I mention this because there may be many readers like me who may feel out of their depth, or inadequate, because they can't identify with such vivid, intense experiences: perhaps I may represent the pint-of-mild brigade?

I think that vocation isn't an external calling, but an internal growing up into oneself; that God is inside me, growing with me (or not growing); that I can never fully know him or myself. But I am increasingly aware in a new way that I need him enormously; and so searching for God is searching for myself, and vice versa. I think we all need periods of 'doing' which are in fact deserts, preparation times, for the years of 'being'. The 'doing' years are 'Petrine': Peter thought he could follow Christ, fight for him, be loyal to him, under his own steam. He learned the hard way that this isn't possible. The 'being' years are like Peter after the resurrection, on the lakeside in Galilee, conscious that Jesus is everything to him in a new way, yet not sure how to live this new awareness.

So a vocation is a constant wakening up to God and myself: new vistas, new challenges, new fears, new joys and new relationships. We must always be on pilgrimage, on the move. So many monks, so many married people, get bogged down, bored with themselves and life. They no longer feel the same about themselves (their vocation, their marriage, their job, their community) as they did in their twenties, and this can be unsettling. A junior monk said to me the other day, 'If I take solemn vows, how do I know that in ten years' time I won't be bored, or find that I have grown into someone so different to what I am now that I will go off and get married?' The short answer is: No one knows. And this is what a vocation should be: a journey into the unknown, with God.

I also think that the past few years have begun to give me (in glimpses) an experiential insight into the *way* God loves. He *never* demands more than I can give; he never ties me up with gossamer threads of possessiveness; he never sulks or tries to gain my affection by little attentions. He leaves me utterly free to be, to be myself, to love in my way. I am learning to love in this way, or, rather, I now see that this is the divine way of loving: to make no demands, as of right, on the community or friends. I want, in a way I never have before, to love and pray and live without asking for satisfaction in return. It's painful, but so liberating, and I thank God for letting me begin to share in his way of loving. I suppose our Lady is the living embodiment of just loving without making any demands whatsoever on God or on anyone, just resting in the Lord. This is, of course, what all parents have to do as their children grow up and leave the nest; but how hard it is for them and how much they need help.

The second point that struck me in the Odysseys is the way people have gone on searching for God, for love, for an understanding of themselves and others. This is tremendous and shows great integrity and a true grasp of our baptismal vocation. I got rather stuck and ossified in my headmagisterial job and leaving it has been the quickening of me (and incidentally of the school too!). Monastic life must be nomadic at heart, a search for the unpredictable God who dances elusively ahead of us, beckoning, calling, never standing still. I'm always trying to catch him with a butterfly net so that I can pin him as an exhibit on my map of life. Now I realize I can't, he won't let me, and this is exhilarating and liberating. Thank God for God.

Yet to be nomadic at heart, always wanting to catch God and to see what is over the next hill, shouldn't be a restless, frenetic process. St Benedict so wisely warns the abbot (and every monk) against becoming 'zelotypus', that is, consumed by a kind of anxious perfectionism. My baptismal vocation seems to me to be the grace to go on searching for God all my life and to do this in the company of Jesus: sounds daft, but the God in me is finding his way back to God in himself. Integrity is not letting myself get sidetracked or bogged down on this voyage of discovery. Like Christ, we have nowhere to lay our heads, so I mustn't go to sleep en route and dream of the past. For many monks the alluring siren of the past is *the* seductress of the monastic life: no change, no upsetting of my daily rhythm, my relationships, my sense of security. Monks and layfolk, if they are Christian, must always look to the future, to the resurrection.

One cause of the Jews' blindness to Christ was their inability to worship the God of today who is beckoning us forward to his tomorrow. They looked back to yesterday and assumed that God was simply the God of their fathers, not a living God for today and tomorrow. Their hope in the future was a form of nostalgia: a hope that God would repeat the past. But he rarely does; he seems to prefer to make all things new. Christ's resurrected life arose out of his life on earth, but it is no repetition of his thirty-three years in Palestine. Continuity and organic growth, yes; but no recycling of the past. This is a vital insight for the development of both the individual and the individual in a community. We must be faithful to the past, to the traditions of our fathers, but we must expect that what will emerge from this fidelity is a new form of life. Too often the individual and the community crush each other through lack of understanding of the new ways into which God is leading them. The same can be true in families as children grow up and strike out on their own. The past can never be repeated or relived as though all we had to do was to thaw it like frozen food and serve an identical meal again.

My third point is about as confused and jumbled as the other two. I find all kinds of longings and yearnings in me that are triggered by my monastic life, but are at the same time stifled by it; and yet I know that they can find resolution and fulfilment only in my living as a monk. I don't know how to find words for this which aren't either too pious-sounding, too profound-sounding or too grandiloquent.

I long to help people find the joy of Christ, to find him in prayer, to enjoy living, for God to come alive in their lives, and yet there doesn't seem to be enough time or opportunity in my way of life here; or I get quickly tired and bored and so let the opportunities slip; or I am fearful or nervous of doing anything. I so much want to give, to love, to pray – and yet I do so little of what I want to do.

I long to love all the community, to know them really, to have an abiding, growing friendship with each and every one, to share in our joint discovery of God: and yet, and yet . . . I don't want to. I don't want to be caught! But I feel that there is in the community a real groundswell of affection and supportive sympathy that is ready like a wave to break all over each one of us. This is exciting, tantalizing and frustrating when it doesn't happen; but I thank God for it. Surely this is part of the hundredfold promised me?

Then there are the friends I have outside the 'walls': there isn't enough time for them or chance to see them enough. And there is Peru: that is a challenge and a beckoning from God to bring all of them into my life.

There is so much going on in the monastic life, so many people, so much to do, so much to absorb in prayer and reading that I find it bewildering in an intoxicated kind of way. I want solitude, companionship, prayer, activity, relaxation and fun, care of souls, all at once and not at all, inextricably mixed together, pressed down and running over. I am for ever finding new facets of myself and of the life.

It has recently struck me how profound and evocative is that sigh of St Augustine: 'O Beauty, so ancient and so new!' That is what I want in community: the steadfastness, security and strength of unchanging relationships, of the rhythm of life, of knowing that God is always there waiting – together with, in the same gulp, a freshness, a new growth, new eyes to look into, new challenges, new insights. O Beauty, so ancient and so new!

Isn't this what we all long for, what we long to possess in God, in our friends, in our families and communities? Lay families can break down through boredom (just concentrating on the old, the familiar, the ancient) or through the zelotypus syndrome which makes them fickle and shallow, always chasing that will o' the wisp, happiness. Monastic communities can also break down for the same reasons. Let us help each other to search for you, Beauty so ancient and so new.

I'm not aware of deep, dark, momentous, earth-shaking experiences in my life. Inside me, I feel pretty ordinary, run-of-the-mill, unadventurous and plain, but I am aware that I have been given – and I can't imagine why – great dollops of affection and kindness and love by many more people than I have ever returned it to. I rejoice in this experience and I suppose it's an experience I long for everyone to bask in; I believe profoundly that it is open to everyone who lives the monastic life.

Lord, you know I come to you in prayer in all sorts of moods and shapes. So often I come to you in duty bound and because I am dutiful and cold I find you academic and cold; Lord, you know that our conversation then is a sort of skirmish, circling around the things that are troubling or irritating or weighing me down. It's all a heavy effort of will and I get bored by you – as you probably are with me. It's like talking to a member of my community who bores me and I feel I ought to talk because he and I have this radical link of belonging to each other. But the heart of me, my inner longings and interests, aren't really met or satisfied, so I leave feeling empty and yet satisfied in that I have done my duty. It's funny, Lord, but so often my prayer is like that.

How I want to be on fire with you and yet I am not. Why? Do I lack faith in you, Lord, as a real living person? I think I do. Am I so steeped in the mess of selfishness that I really have no time for you when you don't seem to give me what I want? I think this is part of the answer. I sometimes wonder – no, fear, but I don't like admitting this very often – that the root cause of my dull, frigid, dutiful praying is the nasty fact that I'm not good at loving, that I have a small heart. I love myself, yes, but can I love you, or indeed anyone, with that reckless absorbing passion that is so giddily wonderful? This reflection makes me curl up, Lord, when what I long for – I think I do truly long for it and it's not just make-believe – is to love you passionately, to hold your feet like Mary Magdalene in the garden and just look at you, saying, 'Rabbi'. Lord, you know that this is what I want but I haven't got this love in me to give you. Lord, I think that what I really want from you in prayer is a huge pulsating heart to love you and other people, live for you and others, be enraptured in you. But I don't seem to have it. I'm not being mock modest, Lord; my heart is small and fickle and you know it. I know this because there are so many things I want that aren't you, and if I don't have them my prayer is no satisfaction and my moods are governed not by you and prayer but by the emptiness I feel.

I think I used to be worried that you didn't seem to answer prayers, for myself, for friends, for all sorts of things large and small, but this doesn't really worry me now. I am often saddened, Lord, that you don't give good health or happiness or faith to the people I'm praying for, but this doesn't make me doubt you. It just makes me realize I don't comprehend you, I don't comprehend how you love others, or me, that you are a stupendous mystery; but I do believe that the only thing you have and can give is love, though I don't understand very often how you give it. You are mysterious.

But I think, Lord – no, I know it – that what you have given me over the years in prayer is a peace that is a yearning. In my inner heart, I am not bored by you at all, and you have helped me to understand, though I do it badly and fitfully as you know too well, how to love you, how to love others, how to work and how to accept myself. You sometimes suffuse all those jealousies and pettinesses, cruelties and lazinesses, that are part of the fibre of my being, with your peace, and I feel you are healing me and helping me to grow into your likeness. I thank you, Lord, that you have transformed and do transform my life. This is a lovely experience. My yearning is to have you do this totally now, though this all too often gets covered up and submerged in daily affairs. But it's there, and I can feel it growing in pain and am frustrated when it's not growing.

I think, Lord, that what you give me and everyone in prayer is a new vision, or a new dimension. The people I am fond of and love, the things I like doing, the places I like, are in some intangible way different, added to, increased by you. You don't possess or own anyone or anything in an obsessive, grasping, desperately clutching way, and this tender compassion is what you are slowly giving me in prayer, and it's wonderful. The people and places and activities (like golf!) which I love and like become different in you. The threats, menaces, pangs of loss and absence somehow don't matter when lapped around in your peace and your yearning, even though they hurt. But they hurt in a new way, the way you give us when you say, Let not your hearts be troubled. And this is a wonderful revelation and I thank you for it.

Lord, I may be being heretical or untheological, but I don't mind and you know what I mean, when I say that your abiding presence – yes, that's it, Lord, prayer is your abiding presence made real – somehow takes the sting out of my sins. They matter but they also don't matter, because of you.

What I long for is for others, for everyone, to persevere in praying, in letting you yearn and groan and doubt and rejoice in *their prayer. I want you to come alive in others so that they can taste and see you and have another vision and dimension in their living. In all the sorrow and bitterness and heaviness of heart I see in people, I yearn for them to find you in prayer. You don't make the pain or the problems less, but you make them different, you transform them. And this, Lord, is your peace. Please give it.*

I don't know where all this outpouring has taken me, it's so full of 'I', but I think it's shown me that prayer means that you come alive in the heart of everyone who prays. Your Spirit begins to take over and it's through you living, struggling to breathe in me, yearning, that I am coming to realize, in odd moments, that it is in prayer that we live and move and have our being.